# The
# Dharmic Challenge

*Putting
Sathya Sai Baba's Teachings
into Practice*

Compiled & Edited by Judy Warner

**L**EEL**A** INC.
PRESS
*A Non-Profit Corporation*
Faber, VA

First published in 1995 by
Leela Press Inc.
4026 River Road
Faber, VA  22938

Library of Congress No. 95-077771

The Dharmic Challenge: putting Sathya Sai Baba's teachings into practice
/compiled and edited by Judy Warner.


Cover Photo:  Kekie Mistry


ISBN 0-9629835-6-X


Typeset in 12 point Times Roman
Printed in the United States of America by BookCrafters

Dedicated with love and devotion

to

**Bhagavan Sri Sathya Sai Baba**

By the Same Author

*Transformation of the Heart*

# TABLE OF CONTENTS

# ACKNOWLEDGMENTS

I would like to express my gratitude to:

Meg Lundstrom for her help in copyediting this book, as well as for her additional help with creative editing.

Mimi Goldberg for her help with reviewing and editing these stories.

Marya Kivistik who found more errors and places to improve when I gave her the finished manuscript to read.

Jay Borden for his workshop entitled "Business is business - for Profit?" which inspired the idea for this book.

Sathya Sai Baba. Without His grace, none of these stories could have been written nor would this book have been published.

**Note:** All quotations, unless otherwise identified, are from Sathya Sai Baba.

# INTRODUCTION

*The Dharmic Challenge* is a compilation of stories from Sathya Sai Baba devotees, based on their personal experiences. The authors describe how they wrestle with the challenge of living by Baba's teachings, their frustrations, growth, successes, and failures.

The question I posed to the authors was, "How can we be *dharmic* in the workplace and in our personal lives?" The challenge is that in society today, people work primarily for power and money. It is considered acceptable, even desirable, to do almost anything to achieve these ends. As Baba devotees, we know the ends do not justify the means. How we perform in business affects how we are at home and vice versa. The overall challenge is to follow Swami's teachings in all aspects of our lives.

The definitions of dharma are many, for there are many levels to dharma. Each author has chosen to deal with the subject in his or her own way. The hope is that these stories will address the subject from varying viewpoints, such as duty, right action, and following one's inner voice, thereby enabling the reader to contemplate this profound challenge in an often inhospitable society.

May this book provoke you into considering your own issues surrounding dharma and inspire you to dare to do the right thing!

JW

*God is everywhere, in everything, in everyone. All your words, the acts that you do, your duty at home towards son and husband, do it with love. See God in everyone. Have your feet in the world, but your mind in the forest.*

Sathya Sai Baba

# WORKING WITH BABA-CONFIDENCE
## Rajan Govindan

From childhood, I have believed that with mental capacity, hard work, and luck, I could achieve most of what I desired. My definition of desires was material goods and social status. My objective, when I came to the United States twenty-five years ago, was to work hard and be successful in the business world. Through the grace of God, I now have a good job and a healthy family, and I have been reasonably successful in the banking business, where I have gained a modicum of financial stability.

Fifteen years ago, I became a member of our local Sai Baba center. I began reading and hearing about Swami's teachings, but my initial interest was in the melodious *bhajans*.

Back then, I lived in two different worlds. One was "business as usual," and the other was the Sai Baba *satsang*. The values and the kind of socializing in these two worlds were entirely different, and I purposely kept them separate. My life was good and only getting better; therefore, I could see no reason to reform myself. However, as I sat through more study circles and increasingly began to understand Swami's teachings, it began to dawn on me that something was wrong. It was not enough to be a part-time devotee. Rather, I had to change my life to search for and realize the God within. This realization initially led to one of the most depressing periods of my life.

I was born and raised in India in a middle-class family. Through Baba's will and enormous sacrifices on the part of my parents, I had attended graduate school in the States, found jobs, and was finally seeing the "fruits of my labor," or so I thought. Life was going very well for me. I had a job with a good income, a house, cars, a bright family, and a world of material goods within reach. Wasn't that what it was all about? My only concerns were the next promotion, the children's grades, health, and the new fancy upgrades to our material possessions. As long as I had imagination, patience, and time, there were no limits. I was on my way.

At the Baba center, however, the discussions were beginning to seriously affect my way of thinking. It began to dawn on me that none of my worldly goals should be important. On further introspection, it hit me that the end results of these goals, worldly possessions, were not even permanent; they could all be gone tomorrow. By examining events around me, it started to dawn on me that so much of what happened to people was out of their control. The brightest and the hardest-working did not always make it to the top (poor interpersonal skills, I thought); the most successful were suddenly left penniless (bad planning, I thought); the average person who seemed to put in the minimal effort rocketed to the top (family legacy, I thought); the poor and homeless addicts wasted away (laziness, I thought); the most careful driver would be involved in a fatal accident, while the obese individual with the worst eating habits would live forever. I finally began to understand that it was only through God's grace and *karma* that I had all this good fortune. Moreover, even having the opportunity, desire, energy, and ability to be productive was a divine gift. It became clear that possessions were not worth the effort, that I had to look for a more permanent source of happiness.

As you can imagine, all these revelations created an immense amount of confusion and stress. I was unsure how to go about dealing with the conflict going on inside me. I would go to retreats and meet people whom I considered much more realized, yet who would be going through the same struggles that I was encountering. I wondered if I was wasting time spending long hours at work and making personal and family sacrifices when all the effort could have been directed to God-realization. I was on the wrong track, but I didn't know how to stop and change.

I needed the financial compensation to pay the mortgage and send two boys off to college. I needed the career advancement to satisfy the dreaded ego. It felt like I was on a moving treadmill: if I stopped, I would fall off. I couldn't ignore what Baba was saying because, week upon week, the study circles were hammering in the same message: the only purpose of life was God-realization. However, I could not understand what that meant to me specifically or what the formula was to become an evolved soul. I wanted to get there, but I had to figure out my own way.

Initially, my reactions to reading books about Baba had left me feeling more amazed than transformed. The very first, Howard Murphet's *Man of Miracles*, was definitely a thriller that I couldn't put down. However, it was the miracles that intrigued me, not the fact that God was all-powerful and could do whatever He chose to do. I followed this with a series of books describing personal experiences that reinforced my faith that God can make miracles happen, but did little to make me realize the need for faith in God. I then graduated to Baba's *Vahinis[1]*, which were easy to read but extremely complex to internalize. I very conveniently rationalized that much of what I was reading and not understanding was more applicable to those in less "aggressive" pursuits of life, such as teachers, preachers, and social workers. I convinced myself that Baba's message was for those entering the fourth stage of life, that of renunciate. I rationalized that since I was in the householder stage and doing no harm to anyone, I could continue in the same fashion.

Then I heard Dr. John Hislop, one of Swami's first American devotees, speak at one of our regional retreats, and I was sufficiently moved to read his book *My Baba and I*. The message of Baba's that the book forcefully conveyed to me is that the very essence of life, the purpose of each and every action however insignificant, is to evolve to Godliness. This

---

[1]*Vahini* in sanskrit means "stream." These writings are Baba's stream of thought on a range of subjects such as meditation, right action, wisdom, peace and divine love.

just about blew me away. It was not just the bhajans, not just the time I did my praying, not just the time at the center, but everything I did, my every breath, that led toward this evolution.[2] I decided that this was all fine; however, I would go ahead and continue what I was doing until I was ready to retire and maybe come back to Baba's teachings at a later date. But I learned another lesson as well: once Baba hooks you in, He doesn't let you off so easily. He slowly, surely, and sometimes painfully makes you want to change. And I knew my slow and sure transformation had begun.

The next stage of my growth was the hardest and the most painful. I felt an intense internal conflict as I contemplated giving up the "business profession" and taking up a less aggressive and less time-consuming way of life - less influenced by title, wealth, and success and more centered on service activities, meditation, and soul-searching.

While these thoughts were tormenting me, the daily newspapers told of recession, layoffs, declining real-estate prices, unemployment, skyrocketing health care costs, and inflation. My parents had just moved in with us from India, and their care and health insurance costs had to be considered. The reality was that to resign one job meant finding a new one. To sell the house and find a more affordable alternative, maybe a move to India, was not truly feasible since our teenage boys would have been devastated for sure, and they could very well have revolted and asked to stay behind. Either wisdom prevailed, or I rationalized that such a drastic course of correction did not make sense. I kept asking myself over and

---

[2]Baba has said that to lead a meaningful life, we must know where we have come from and the destination we want to reach. Right from the first cry at birth, we are asking the question, "kohum," or Who am I? The answer to the question "kohum" comes from within as we breath 21,600 times a day. As we inhale, we make the sound "so," and when we exhale, we utter the sound "hum" - together, "sohum," which means "He is me." Just as we are born saying "kohum," we must live to the end of our life saying "sohum."

over, "What should I do?"

My continuing emotional struggle and constant introspection have brought me to my current stage of evolution and reasoning.

Firstly, if Baba wanted me to be someone else, He would have done just that. Baba has placed me in my current role at this time and place for a purpose which only He understands. My challenge is to fulfill that role without delusions of grandeur and to dedicate everything to him, a challenge I continue to find hard to practice since I often forget that I am only an instrument of His will.

Secondly, I have obligations to a family given by Him that I am duty-bound to fulfill to the best of my ability: to provide for them, to be a pillar should they need support, and to instill in them the conduct and values defined by Swami. Teaching them values that I have barely learned myself is difficult to do. Like many newly converted parents, I have practiced the credo, "Do as I preach, not as I do." I have learned that showing by example is far more difficult - and far more effective. Our boys are not totally convinced of our belief in Baba. We have nurtured and encouraged their independent thinking, so their lack of faith shouldn't bother me, but it does. But I am slowly realizing they belong to Swami and He will do what's best for them. The important thing is whether we have instilled in them the self-confidence that Baba would have us teach them.

In my never-ending quest for enlightenment, let me tell you how I deal with what I call the three components of my life: the professional world, my domestic or family life, and the spiritual umbrella that covers and brings these two together.

The fundamental goal of a business person appears to be to satisfy the shareholders' desire to build wealth, yet Swami's strongest message to me is to help mankind. In business, a manager's prime motivation and responsibility is to achieve the corporation's goal for profits by optimizing its resources, which is mostly human capital. Before Baba's influence mellowed me, I was able to deal with people issues based on measurements

and well-defined objectives. Now however, the evaluation
process has become very complicated. As soon as I see God in
another person, conflict takes over. What should I do about a
"good" person not wanting or able to do their job and produce
results? How long do I continue to cajole, encourage or even
plead (and pray) before taking some radical action? The more
difficult question becomes: Who am I to judge? My corporation
says it's my job, yet doesn't Baba say we shouldn't judge
another?

I have rationalized my response to this dilemma by drawing
some parallels to Krishna's advice to Arjuna on the eve of the
big battle of Kurukshetra. My job in the corporation is my
battlefield. I have to play out my part and do my duty. If I
cannot do that, I should resign and do something that does not
require such evaluations and decisions. Since I decided to
accept this as my role, I have had to make judgments, but I try
to make them without ego or prejudice or a false sense of
power. I try very hard to concentrate on the quality and
quantity of the efforts of the individuals and not **on** the
individuals themselves, albeit the fine line does get blurred
from time to time. I do what I believe is right for Baba who,
in my mind, takes on the role of my employer. Most times a
prayer to Baba helps me at least verify that my decisions are
not coming from my ego, but rather from my understanding of
my duty. However, even with all this analysis, contemplation,
and rationalization, I am not always comfortable with who I am
and what I am doing.

Some of the very same conflicts arise when I am working on
a competitive bid for new business. Sometimes when we are
trying to strategize how to package our strengths and hide our
weaknesses, it borders on not being totally honest. Being a
member of Baba's team, I would never condone lying, so I get
my colleagues to focus on our strengths. Usually Swami gets
my clients totally captivated by our strengths. However, there
are times when I feel we are compromising the truth; then I
withdraw myself from the team and tend to forget my duty as

their leader. I know I cannot hide from my appointed duty, but I also know I must work out an effective, acceptable, and honest approach.

I am working hard to perform my duty without worrying about the result and thinking, "What's in it for me?" After years of training and mind conditioning that taught me to focus on such results as college grades and job promotions and raises, it is hard to break the habit of worrying about the rewards for my efforts. The biggest reason for this concern seems to be due to my attachment and to commitments built up as I have gone along: college tuition for the kids, mortgage for the house, planning for retirement. I recognize that if I had total faith in Swami and trust that He would always take care of me, I wouldn't have to worry about the future. Although I am trying, I am not yet this evolved.

My family and I have established budgets to put a ceiling on our desires as well as to contribute more and more of what Baba gives us to those in need. However, the challenge for me is to give without feeling guilty or feeling that to give is a requirement. Unfortunately, I also continue to want frivolous items, and so I have developed a financial incentive to curb these desires: I donate equal value to charity every time I waste money on a useless object. Doubling the ante is a pretty effective curb on desires!

Sometimes when I look at myself, I am humbled by how much success I have had in my professional and family life. I am convinced that this is only because of Baba's will. Initially, the feeling that my destiny was in Baba's hands rather than my own was frightening, but now I am able to accept success and failure, boss and subordinate, reward and penalty, with more equanimity. I now believe that what Baba gives, He gives for a purpose. It is important to treat what Baba has given wisely and without attachment. There is no question that each of us would define "wisely" in different terms. To me, it entails humility and gratefulness and, mostly, not to show off success or feel guilty about it.

As I struggle along my path, I am slowly but surely developing a sense of *Baba-confidence.* This is my definition of seeing my Baba within myself and gradually developing a sense of Self-confidence. This assures me that as long as I do my duty according to my conscience and do it with discipline and devotion, the Baba within will be able to cope with the future, whatever it may bring.

I am constantly working to dedicate all my actions to Baba. I used to take credit personally for all my successes and attribute only failures to God's will. Now I am able to dedicate the wins also to Swami. But more importantly, I am able to remember to dedicate my actions to Him before I take on any action. The more significant and complex the transaction or business becomes, the harder I think of Baba. The most amazing result is that I have never lost, although I have not necessarily won every time: the important point is that I have felt good about most of the outcomes. But sometimes when things don't work out right, I forget and think and believe that I could have controlled the events. In these instances, I lose my Baba-confidence and begin to question my actions and my ability. Once again, I worry about everything.

The good news is that I am soon able to focus on Baba and remind myself that the result was what Baba had in mind, and most importantly, that I cannot do anything about what has already happened. Second-guessing only makes me depressed. I soon realize that, as I did my best, the result is what Swami wanted, and the anxiety leaves me.

The last, but probably the most important application of Baba's teachings to my professional life, is how I conduct myself at all times in terms of objectives, associates, values, conduct, food, thought, and everything else. Clearly I want to be always good in my dialogue, appearance, thinking, and consumption. But Baba, recognizing the conflicts of modern-day life, has made it just a bit easier for me. He has said that for those of us involved in the business world, He expects us to be 70 percent *sattwic* (pure, calm), 20 percent *rajasic* (emotional, active), and 10 percent *tamasic* (lazy, undiscriminating). The challenge, of course, is to measure whether I am achieving the 70 percent goal and to strive to be 100 percent sattwic. It is amazing how conscious dedication of every task to Baba can simplify the job of measuring. Somehow 100 percent can even seem attainable.

Through Swami's grace, I have a wonderful family, all in good health, a nice home and an interesting job that keeps me busy and helps pay the bills. By and large, circumstances and life's events have been good to us. I think Baba has His invisible fence around us that prevents us from getting into trouble. I feel truly blessed to be born in the golden age of Sai. I should say doubly blessed, because Baba has held tight the reins even as I tried to turn away and do "my" thing.

I should be happy and jumping for joy. Doesn't Baba tell us that He wants us to "Enjoy" and "Be happy"? But the truth is I am not always happy, and I often wonder why. I think the answer lies in my failure to dedicate all my thoughts and actions to Baba and my failure to always have 100 percent faith in God, which often causes me to fret about the outcome. Clearly this shows that I have not yet fully internalized the notion that everything is Baba's will and I am merely an actor in this play of life.

Swami tells us that one of the best ways to feel we are one with Him is to do service. Over the years, with Baba's persuasive hand, I have started to pay more attention to the needs of the less fortunate. When first doing service, I used to have the superior feeling of being the provider. I believed I was doing it for "them." But with constant pounding from Baba to see God in all, to look people in the eye with a smile, not to judge others, not to question why people were not doing something for themselves, I began to change. I am beginning to learn to do things for others, especially those not connected to me in any earthly way, without expectations of results or rewards. It no longer matters if they are family, friend, enemy, boss or subordinate. I realize that so little separates the "haves" from the "have-nots," so quickly can our roles change. I need to find ways to happily and selflessly share more of my Baba-time, Baba-experiences, and Baba-money that He has so generously given me. This will help me overcome my ego, which tends to always want more.

Swami's teachings and rules may be easy to understand, but I find them hard to follow, harder yet to practice in a modern-day business enterprise. As I grow older and, I hope, wiser, I experience so many things in life that are hard to rationalize or explain. Before Baba so forcefully entered my life, I found success so sweet and well-deserved, and I always wanted more and the trappings that went with it. If things didn't go my way, which was at least half the time, I blamed everybody else and, in my own egotistical way, felt angry at the powers that be for not recognizing and rewarding my special skills and contribution. I would not only be angry but sad, insecure, and sometimes irrational.

Now when things don't work out as I expect, I understand the rule of karma and know that Baba is with me all the time. And realizing that the results are in Swami's hands, I see that there is no good or bad outcome. Understanding this makes working and living so much easier. I continue to work as hard and as intelligently as I can, because that is my duty assigned by Baba. I know that with Swami in control, there is no way I could lose at anything. I realize now that feeling happy or sad is not what it is all about for me, but rather it is the quest to do better with my life day by day and ultimately to realize as Swami says:

*Life is a game, play it.*
*Life is a challenge, meet it.*
*Life is Love, live it.*
*Life is a dream, realize it.*

# BECOMING SPIRITUAL LIONS
## Linda Upadhyaya

I will never forget the day I was waiting at the outpatient alcoholism clinic to be interviewed for a job as counselor. I was sitting there in my typical interview clothes, smiling politely to the other employees and thinking about what this job would be like. I remembered being in school where the teachers actually tried to talk us out of going into this field of alcoholism counseling. Many of the lecturers warned us that with chemically dependent people, we would meet a lot of anger and resistance to treatment. I didn't take it very seriously at the time because I was in the safety of the school environment. As I was waiting to be called, I thought about Swami, and wondered if he, too, wanted me to do this work. The philosophy of Alcoholics Anonymous is directly in line with Baba's teachings: it is a very honest, spiritual program where people work on themselves to recover and eventually help others to do the same. I felt that anyone who followed the Twelve Steps of A.A. would have an extremely enriched life, with God as the focus. It felt right to be sitting there; I was happy and at ease as I thought about the Lord.

Suddenly I was bolted out of my reverie by a screaming counseling session that was in progress in the next room. The counselor was actually yelling and using profanities at the client, while the client defensively screamed back using the same language. Then the door flew open and the client stormed out of the office past me as I smiled uncomfortably and said "hello." She looked at me deadpan and walked past without a word. Then the counselor came out of the office, with a cigarette hanging from her lips, looking very tough. I know my eyes were wide open as I watched. Before I could gather myself together, the client reappeared and they went back into the office where they continued their session, loudly.

"Okay, Lord, I'm out of here!" I screamed inside to Swami. I was really frightened. Most of the patients I had worked with up until this point were psychiatric, mostly chronic schizophrenics who functioned at a minimal level. They were the "unwanted leftovers of society" and were surprised and happy just to receive a friendly "hello" and a smile, especially since many were used to receiving nothing. "Baba," I cried, "I can't work here. I'm used to over-medicated, docile psychiatric patients who hardly talk at all! These clients will eat me alive! Swami, help! I don't want this job even if they offer it to me." Reluctantly, I added, "...unless it is Your Will."

After a grueling half-hour interview, where I felt I answered most questions wrong but I didn't care, I was absolutely shocked when I was offered the job. And I was even more shocked when I heard myself accept! It was clear to me, however, that this was what Swami wanted. Despite my fear, I remembered that He says, "Whatever you do, wherever you are placed, believe that God has put you there for that work."

I have believed in Sathya Sai Baba since 1979, and I feel that He does put us all wherever we need to be for our growth. Swami tells us, "Start the day with love. Spend the day with love. Fill the day with love. End the day with love. That is the way to God." To me this means that I should **always** be gentle and kind. The experience of this job, however, is teaching me that love comes in many forms and therefore to appear gentle and kind are not always appropriate. As time goes on, I see that I need to learn how to be stronger and more assertive in order to really put Swami's teachings into practice and not to allow others or circumstances to control me. In fact, I know that Swami put me in this career to toughen me up. I am sometimes afraid that I may get too toughened, and I need to be balanced in this. Love must always be the motive in my interventions with clients. Just as Swami sometimes appears to be very tough and powerful, or even angry, He is always pure love and gives us just what we need to get closer to him.

Swami is constantly placing me in situations where I not only learn to be strong and assertive, but where I can learn how to treat each client in the best possible way. There have been many hard and painful lessons for me, and also wonderful ones. Swami tells us:

*Without self-confidence, no achievement is possible. If you have confidence in your strength and skill, you can draw upon the inner springs of courage and raise yourselves to a higher level of joy and peace. For confidence in yourselves arises through the Atma, which is your inner reality. The Atma is peace, it is joy, it is strength, it is wisdom. So it is from the Atma that you draw all these equipments for spiritual progress.*

I was 19 years old when I first became devoted to Sai Baba. I was brought up Jewish and was taught that belief in a form of God is equivalent to idol worship. It was a very painful and exhilarating process to accept the idea that God **can** have a form, that He is actually alive today! I am grateful for that pain now. Because of the tremendous resistance of my parents, I feel that I was able to look deeply into Swami to work through the idea that this could be possible, that He could be God.

One day I innocently and excitedly told my parents, "God is on earth, alive!" I wanted to spread the news. Wouldn't everybody want to know? What could be more important? I thought it would be a disservice **not** to tell. Well, as you can guess, the news was not received with joy and ecstasy. My parents thought I had joined a cult and that the devil was stealing me away. To this day, they despise my involvement with Swami. They almost disowned me for my belief in Him, and I was therefore forced to take Him very seriously. Of course, it is only through the Lord's grace that we develop faith, and I know that He called me. It wasn't I who accepted Him.

At that time, I had enormous difficulty defending myself. Everything that came out of my mouth regarding Swami made me sound like a brainwashed child. I knew and experienced Him as God, but I could not express myself maturely and confidently. My parents became scared and furious. I couldn't seem to back up my views (How can anyone **prove** or even attempt to explain who Swami is?) and I was much too open and vulnerable. And it hurt me to hear them insult my Lord.

I feel that this experience is one of the reasons I have difficulty being assertive with others. At that time, I believed that spirituality meant never fighting back, but rather taking whatever came my way graciously, no matter how painful. I was therefore seen as a doormat, a weak person by my parents, and I was not taken seriously. Even before this, I was never assertive because I never had to be. I always did the "right" thing in order to get their approval and love. The deeper I look into Swami's teachings, the more I realize that He doesn't want us to allow others to control us; He wants us to be strong "spiritual lions."

*"If God wills" means only if you assert your own all-powerful will. The solution is therefore to awaken the inherent power and splendor of your soul. Do it. You are verily the immortal Truth, the great, deathless, and changeless Reality. Be victory ever yours.*

I work in a rough, inner-city neighborhood where the crime rate is high and there is rampant drug abuse, predominantly of crack, cocaine, heroin, marijuana, and alcohol. About 95 percent of my clientele consists of people who have not graduated from high school (some are illiterate), who have never been employed, who are on public assistance, and who are extremely angry about being in treatment. Most of the time their treatment is mandated by probation or parole officials, by the child welfare administration, or by the welfare system. Very few come voluntarily with a desire to free themselves of addiction, and most feel they don't really have a drug or alcohol problem. They therefore direct their anger toward their counselors, because their counselors are in contact with the mandating agencies. To establish a good working relationship with a client, then, is often a long and tedious process. People can only benefit from help if they want it or come to realize they need it.

One of my clients, Ann, was a beautiful black woman about my age, a severe crack addict, and alcoholic. She had been a prostitute in Manhattan for years, and she had three young children in foster care. The moment I saw Ann and completed the initial interview, I was afraid I would be unable to handle her. She was tough, angry, and very intelligent, and I was intimidated by her. When she looked at me, I could see she was happy to have this innocent-looking "white girl" as her counselor: I'm exactly the type of person Ann thought she could manipulate. And she was absolutely right! I have a round face and look young for my age, which makes the job even tougher for me. It is assumed I know nothing about my clients' lifestyles, can't possibly identify with them and would believe anything I'm told; that is how I look!

I asked my supervisor to transfer Ann to another counselor, but was told that she would remain my client. I knew it was my responsibility to set the tone immediately, setting limits from the start. Ann and I had a very tumultuous relationship, and I'm sure that my ambivalence didn't help. When she happened to be in a good mood and felt safe enough, we would get along famously. She would share feelings about her life, her family, her relationships, and even knock on my door to talk some more when it wasn't her normal session time. In retrospect, I realize this was not good for her treatment: she needed structure. At those times, though, I thought we had really connected, that we had a good, honest working relationship and that, surely, she was on the road to recovery. Then suddenly, with no warning, she would either miss her appointments or become verbally abusive toward me. I knew it was because she was scared; she probably felt she had gotten too close to me and needed to create some distance. Still, I took it personally and felt hurt and frightened. I allowed her to be in control of her treatment. A year passed before I was able to work effectively with Ann.

Alcoholics often requires direct confrontation. Manipulation and unconscious denial of the problem are large aspects of this disease of addiction. Being "nice" is not helpful. It may enable them to continue to drink and use drugs that are extremely harmful. The disease will eventually kill them if it is not taken seriously. I learned this the hard way, and Ann was one of my teachers.

Ann had suddenly stopped attending groups and sessions with me, and after several attempts to contact her, I decided to close her case. I asked my supervisor to sit in on the session in which I would tell Ann the status of her situation. On the day that she finally showed up, her attitude was really unendurable. She was very abusive and hostile toward me and was yelling at my supervisor about me as if I weren't even in the room. I began to get furious. The anger was growing in my stomach. I felt like I wanted to kill her. After all the hard work we had done together, how could she be so mean and deceitful? I prayed to be able to handle this therapeutically and calmly (the way I thought Swami would like me to), but I was unable to control myself. I began yelling and cursing at her about her attitude and lack of respect. I was shaking with anger and almost started crying. Even my supervisor was unable to intervene. Suddenly, Ann stopped. She began to smile. And I was sure I understood why. She was smiling because she had realized that she couldn't manipulate me any longer, that I knew her better than she had thought, that I was serious about closing her case. And she didn't want this to happen. Obviously, I could have been firm in a more loving way that day with Ann, but one beneficial aspect of that session was that Ann knew I was serious.

From then on we had a relatively good and honest working relationship. My fear of her began to diminish along with my "niceness," and she began to respect me as her counselor.

Had I been more structured and confrontive from the start and taken better control of her treatment, rather than letting fear motivate me, I may have been more successful with her and I wouldn't have had to lose control. My fear kept me from doing the right thing.

It is clear in this situation that "tough love" was needed, but it is often difficult for me to confront clients. Generally, I can feel when I am being manipulated, but I have a hard time being assertive and strong. When they are swearing and shouting, I find it especially scary. However, fear should never be the motivator of our actions. Swami tells us:

*Wipe out the root causes of anxiety and fear and ignorance. Then only can the true personality of man shine forth. Anxiety is removed by faith in the Lord, the faith that tells you that whatever happens is for the best and that the Lord's will be done.*

I am faced with many kinds of situations through the day, and although it is extremely difficult for me to see what is correct at the time, it is often crystal clear after the fact. One of the greatest lessons that I have learned, and that Ann has taught me, is that acting nice and sweet and understanding, which I thought was spiritual, is not generally the best method to handle alcoholics and substance abusers. This is not to say that we should not have love and understanding or that every counselor must be hard and tough in order to treat the disease, but that we must give the right medicine to each person. Each client requires his or her own unique treatment.

I realize more and more that as a counselor my feelings toward a client can have a major impact on the effectiveness of treatment. In order to act correctly and professionally, my feelings should never interfere with giving a client the best possible treatment. I am learning that any strong emotion, positive or negative, can adversely affect their treatment. Swami says, "Be alike to everyone," and this is a real challenge for me. I find if I really like a client a lot, I can be much too easy-going and unconsciously allow more manipulation, which may enable my client to drink and take drugs. If I really dislike a client, I can become overly confrontive, overly structured, and even distrustful of the person. "Seek out your faults and others' merits," Baba tells us, but it is hard not to judge. I must remember:

> *There may be differences among men in physical strength, financial status, intellectual acumen, but all are equal in the eyes of God; all have the right and potentiality to achieve the goal of merging in him. Note that everyone, from the beggar to the billionaire, is prompted by the urge to achieve Ananda, Supreme Bliss, based on inner peace, unaffected by ups and downs. Every activity, however elementary or earth-shaking, is subservient to this ideal.*

Swami tells us again and again that we are all one. So who am I to know whether a person is likeable or not? Who am I to judge? I have found that appearances are deceiving. The toughest-looking person can be the gentlest pussycat. For example, Joe was a 28-year-old white man who was mandated to treatment by the court for allegedly raping his two daughters while under the influence of heroin and alcohol. As I was taking his initial history, I was disgusted by the thought of working with a rapist, even though he denied the charge, and felt it would be impossible for me to treat him. Again, I asked my supervisor to transfer him to someone else, and again the answer was no. As I got to know Joe, I saw that this man was abused all of his life, had never had any family support or love, and was really a person who needed a lot of care and love, which I eventually was able to give him. He consequently opened up to me in return. Had I remained judgmental toward him, we would never have been able to work together. Swami tells us to "detach with love" but it took a while for me to be able to do this. He says:

*Develop compassion, sympathy, engage in service, understand the agony of poverty and disease, distress and despair; share both tears and cheers with others. That is the way to soften the heart and help sadhana to succeed.*

It is very difficult to counsel people without attachment. If I'm attached to the fruits, I may think that it is because of me or what I have done that a person recovered, when in fact we can only, with God's grace, help ourselves. I know I need to put in the best effort and dedicate the session to Swami, try to keep Him in mind, and realize that the outcome has nothing to do with me. My duty lies in doing the best I can, which for me often means acting confident and assertive rather than kind and sweet, and in learning to see clearly each situation I face. To be able to be strong and structured with an Ann or nonjudgmental and understanding with a Joe - that is my challenge.

Doing this counseling over the last three and a half years has not only helped me be better at my work, but has affected and improved my personal relationships with family and friends. I seem to have gained more self-confidence in every area of my life, but I still have far to go.

Lord Sai, I pray that you continue to strengthen me as your devotee in every situation in my life. Give me the opportunity to please you by doing that which you prescribe. Give me the eyes to see clearly and the ability to perform accordingly, for I have so much to learn, and your Divine Grace to win.

*"Everything has emerged from truth. Truth is the form of the Divine. Everything is based on truth. There is no greater dharma than truth."*

Sathya Sai Baba

# GROWING UP
## Batsheva

So, what is dharma anyway? Since I've come to Swami I've been asking myself this question, but it's like trying to grab a hold of running water. Every time I think I've got "it," it slips out of my hands, and I can hear Swami inside telling me that once I think I've got "it," I've lost "it." With Swami's help, I have been attempting to understand my journey with living dharma.

I was 25 years old when I first came to Sai Baba. I had done so much in my life already. I had grown up in New York City. In high school and college, I'd hung out in all the hippest nightclubs and done the whole life that went with that. After college, I was quickly promoted to running a small publishing company on my own and did well fast.

By the time I got to Sai Baba, I was pretty depressed. I felt I'd already done it all. What was left to do? Life seemed so empty. I had just recently started going to 12-step addiction programs and doing yoga and was just starting to experience God in my life, but I wanted a teacher, a mother, a father, a family. I wanted love.

From the first moment in Sai Baba's presence, I remember feeling totally vulnerable. Suddenly, this 25-year old who had felt so old felt like a baby. All the grown-up things I'd experienced in my life at home no longer seemed to matter. Those old shells, old identities, began to melt off of me. So who was I without all those old trappings? I began to ask these questions and experience how out of touch I really was with myself. For example, I went to buy some saris and watched in awe as the shopkeeper threw reams of different colored materials on the floor. I knew how people dressed in night clubs and in business offices, but how did I really want to dress? What did I like? I didn't know, and for me this showed how far I felt from myself.

About a week into the trip, Swami called me and my stepfather, to whom I was not close, in for an interview. "Who are you with?" Swami kept asking me. I got up and started to leave the room, for I didn't know the answer. Who am I with? I queried myself after this amazing interview. I had no sense of connection to myself, to my family, to anyone or anything, except now I had Sai Baba, who gave me the courage to ask those questions of self-inquiry. Who am I? Where am I from? Where am I going?

I took these questions literally at first. My mother and stepfather left the ashram and I was there alone to ponder. I felt so distant from everyone and so much wanted to be part of a family. I had met this beautifully warm and loving couple a few days before and had a strong feeling that I wanted to know them better. I wrote this in my journal, walked back to my room, and found a note on my door that my room had been changed. I packed up and moved, and awoke the next morning to find that I was in a room a few doors away from these people! Swami!

This couple took me into their lives for the next few years as if I were their daughter and gave me a family and love that I had never experienced before. With them I felt some sense of belonging, for the first time. In the years that I was with them, I allowed myself to discover and express many of the feelings, especially anger, that I had never dared express when I was growing up.

After a while though, I started to notice that I had gotten used to feeling angry and hurt, almost as if this were a new identity - "messed-up and wronged New York City kid without a loving family." One day I realized that this identity was no longer right for me. Even though I had been loved and supported completely during those years by the couple, after awhile I felt limited, boxed in, even by all the love and support. Now, I was ready to find this love for myself and not depend on others for it. Swami had given me what I had prayed for - family and belonging - and now it was time to move on and out of this old identity. Another layer came off.

At this time, I had also gotten interested in understanding my Jewish heritage, something I had not been exposed to as a child. During my first trip in India, I was met by one particular beggar every day in the street. She fixated on me. I, being the Upper East Side New York woman, would ignore her and try not to look at her. She was deformed, dirty, and poor, while I was rich and had everything. I felt ashamed and scared to face her. However, there was no escaping her, for she seemed to sense how I felt. One day, she got more assertive and walked in front of me begging for money and, at that moment, I looked into her eyes and saw that she was glowing. Yes, she was deformed and dirty and poor on the outside, but I caught a glimpse of her inside - she was rich, not I. She was confident, not I. She knew her dharma in life: she was a beggar in India. I did not know mine. In that instant, I knew that I was the poor one. I certainly didn't share in that glow or confidence. What was my country? Who are my people? I had no idea. This is when I deeply felt Baba's message, "Go to the heart of your own religion."

I went to see Swami for His 65th birthday. Within a few weeks, I received the inner guidance to move to Israel, and so I did on January 15, 1991, the first day of the Gulf War. I arrived in the Tel Aviv airport and was greeted by reporters from the *Jerusalem Post*. "How come you are moving to Israel today? Aren't you afraid?" they asked. I gave them a unique story, I suppose, as they quoted me saying, "I believe in God more than politics." Then I told them about my journey with Baba, and how He had directed me to go back to my roots and be with my people. I knew that Swami had sent me to Israel, so I had nothing to fear.

In Israel, I threw myself into the culture. I was thirsty and excited to learn everything about Jewish people and religion. I felt so happy inside to have connected with "my" people. I learned Hebrew in six months, and then moved to a small city in Northern Israel - Safed, the City of Mysticism - to study Kabbalah, Jewish mysticism. I was thrilled to find that there are so many similarities between Swami's teachings and the Kabbalah. In a year's time, I had immersed myself in the Orthodox Jewish world, hearing in the back of my mind Baba's teaching, "Go back to your roots and love your religion with all your heart and soul."

I married a man like me, an American new to religion and open to all faiths, or so I believed. I soon learned that I was mistaken. He chose to go deeper into the mainstream ultra-Orthodox world and deny other religions. I attempted to live this religious life with him to make the marriage work. At his request, I took off the pendant that Swami had materialized for me, hid my books and photos, and stopped all talk of Baba. "He's inside me and I don't need the form," I rationalized, but soon it became very limiting and unhappy for me as I was throwing away what I believed. It became clear that I was not being true to myself, for I could not express my love for Swami and all faiths in the way I wanted.

During this time, I went through tremendous turmoil and questioning. I doubted myself for not being able to stay strong like the few others I knew and loved who were able to stay religious and live in Israel and yet not be affected by the pressures of the mainstream orthodoxy. However, this pressure lived in my house, so I had to face it day in and day out. I questioned everything, especially Baba: perhaps I was crazy and Baba wasn't the divine being that I had believed. My faith was tested so many times. I became confused and unable to think clearly. I did know, though, that in my heart I wasn't happy and that I had to leave this marriage. In time, I realized that there are some people who are religious and yet stay open to other religions, for they are able to focus on love and self-realization as the goal. However, I didn't feel strong enough inside to do this, so I wrote Swami for help.

It soon became clear to me that I was ready to get a divorce. My divorce was no small miracle of Baba's, for it can be very difficult for women to get divorced in Israel. I will never forget my ex-husband yelling in the courtroom to the judges, who are rabbis, "She has a guru in India who she believes is God." Everyone gasped, because I appeared to be a typical religious woman - I wore a long skirt and long sleeves in the heat of the summer and I covered my hair with a scarf, as all religious married women do. Everyone looked at me in disbelief for an answer. "He is absolutely right. I have a guru in India," I confirmed. "We need to talk to you about this," exclaimed a rabbi. "This isn't a Jewish concept!" The rabbis wanted to speak to me about this guru more than about the divorce. At that moment, I looked down at the court reporter and noticed that all our files and his pen were orange - the color of Swami's robe. Baba was there! And by His Grace, I had a smooth and easy divorce proceeding.

I left Israel knowing that I would probably not be returning to live there again. I cried on the airplane, for I loved my new-found country, religion, and heritage, and yet I knew that I had to leave them. I suddenly understood that one of the reasons that Swami had sent me there was to show me how I could get so caught up in identities like being a good wife and a good Jew. When I did this, then I forgot myself and lost my connection to God.

From Israel, I went to India to see beloved Baba and, again, I found new clarity about my dharma. It was time to let go of the past, "Past is passed," and to let go of the outer search. I had looked for family, country, and religion on the outside to find my dharma, my Self, and although I learned and grew a lot, they were only parts of me; they were not my Self.

So now what was my dharma? To do good in the world and act righteously? I had done that before Swami, even in the publishing company, and then as a good wife, and then as a good Jew, but those were just steps; they didn't make me feel closer to God or love. As the layers started to come off, I began to see that my dharma kept changing and that I must constantly uncover my dharma to reveal my true self.

> *"We must first try to understand what Dharma is, then we can try to know our own Dharma or Swadharma... The Swadharma means the path of the Brahman or the path of the Supreme Being... This means that in carrying out one's own Dharma, even if one perishes, it is far better than taking to dharma not belonging to oneself. The latter path is beset with fear."*

At first in my life I had been a cool New York chick, then a successful editor, then a depressed and angry person searching for belonging, then a Jew: all of these things were my dharma for a period of time. But whenever I grasped at a role or an identity, then I would suddenly not feel happy or well, or some crisis would occur that would break me of this identity that I thought was *me*.

> *"Your duty is to abandon. Abandon all your plans, even the best ones. Abandon all theories you cherish, the doctrines you hold dear, the systems of knowledge that have cluttered your brain, the preferences you have accumulated, the pursuit of fame, fortune, scholarship, superiority. These are all material, objective. Enter into the objective world after becoming aware of the Atma. Then you will realize that all is the play of the Atma."*

I returned to the States a few years ago. I am back with my "old" family, whom I love dearly. I am a "regular" American non-practicing Jew again. I keep recalling the Buddhist adage, "Chop wood and carry water before enlightenment, chop wood and draw water after enlightenment." Not that I'm enlightened, but I feel I've come through a cycle. Swami made me a baby again, then brought me through childhood and youth more consciously. Now I'm a new kind of grown-up, experiencing the same sort of life that I had when I first came to Swami, only now more aware that this is all just a play to bring me closer to my higher self, the Atma. I might be in my "old" world, but life is now a meaningful adventure.

I am just back from Prasanthi Nilayam, where almost daily I wrote letters to Swami. I saw that He would only take my letters when I was being most direct, honest, and real. Many days I'd write, "Oh Beloved Lord, please help me become less attached to worldly things. Please help me to love more and desire less... etc. etc." These letters He *never* took. When I wrote, "Swami, I want to move when I get back to the U.S.A... I want an interview..." something really clear and concrete like that, then He'd take the letter immediately. For me the message is to acknowledge and be where I am now, to be *real*. Even if I'm not textbook "holy" or "spiritual," I feel that Swami would rather I be honest with where I am now.

When I first came to Sai Baba, I thought that being a devotee meant I had to be a certain way and that being spiritual meant that I'd have to give up my desires for food, sex, money, and have total equanimity - becoming like a *sanyasi.* Swami has often asked me, "Where is your husband?" I have meditated on this question quite a bit as I know He is trying to show me something about myself with this repeated question.

By believing that to be a good devotee I must renounce all my desires, I had placed an expectation on myself to be someone I wasn't, and this caused me to lose myself and my connection to God. I saw that the layers of "lies" that I tell myself come in all sorts of forms. I must be truthful with myself and my desire for companionship, love, and intimacy. Perhaps I'm not ready, and never will be in this lifetime, to take on *sanyas.* With this question, "Where is your husband?" Swami reveals to me that I can't jump over my desires and act as if they don't exist. I must first look at my desires honestly so that I can look at who I am.

*"Self-realization is possible only by knowing your own real nature."*

Swami has said, "The Atma is also known as 'Awareness.'" When I am honest and aware of my desires, then I can renounce them and, to my surprise, my desires often do get fulfilled in ways I never could have planned or imagined.

"Swami, I'm angry, I don't like this situation!" When I can say something like that and know what I'm really feeling, then I can take responsibility and grow from there. In the past few years, I've been teaching yoga and running workshops on conscious living. One of the concepts I'm always teaching, which of course I most need to learn, is that the yogic process of making changes involves the three A's - Awareness, Acceptance, Adjustment. With the first A, Awareness, I must be excruciatingly honest with where I'm standing in this moment. I might have a good idea or preference about where I want to be, but I can't get there until I'm honest about where I am now. The second A, Acceptance, guides me to accept where I am now. Sometimes I berate myself, as the monkey mind does, for not being more holy or spiritual or for wanting things to be different, but when I do this, I am not able to move from where I am. After I've practiced Awareness and Acceptance, *then* I can Adjust, make changes and grow. When I can hold onto this, to being *real*, i.e. the path of self-*real*ization, then I feel I am acting in accord with my dharma in that moment.

> *"Your conscience knows the real source of joy; it will prod you towards the right path. Your business is to take it as a 'guide' and not disobey it every time it contradicts your fancy."*

So, now I think (oops, I'm thinking and planning again, already an error) that my dharma is to live as true to myself in each moment as I can. My dharma keeps changing, so my job, my sadhana, is to stay ever aware and alert because "I" really love to think I am all my identities, rather than God. Therefore,

I must keep the mind and emotions as clear as I can so that I can remember God.

Sai Baba speaks to me through one of my favorite musicians, Van Morrison, who sings "Enlightenment... don't know what it is" and to "Let go into the mystery..." The mind keeps wanting to figure out what "it" is. What is enlightenment? What is dharma? Sometimes I am afraid to let go into the mystery of life, of God. How right Swami was when He recently told me in an interview, "Mad monkey mind!" I continue to uncover layer after layer of resistance to just being who I am, just being in my dharma, whatever that may be, in each divine moment.

*"In all worldly activities, you should be careful not to offend propriety, or the canons of good nature; you should not play false to the promptings of the Inner Voice, you should be prepared at all times to respect the appropriate dictates of conscience; you should watch your steps to see if you are in someone else's way; you must be ever vigilant to discover the Truth behind all this scintillating variety. This is the entire Duty of man, your Dharma."*

Sathya Sai Baba

# A PERSONAL INVITATION
Jonathan Roof

Seeing my grandfather sit in his high-backed armchair smoking a sweet-smelling pipe, I knew that all was right in the world. His strong self-confidence assured me that he had matters well under control. Indeed, the stately opulence of his home spoke more eloquently than words ever could. He appeared to my young eyes to be one who had clearly achieved mastery of his own world.

From the time I was six or seven, an awareness grew in me that my grandparents enjoyed more than common wealth. My grandfather was a co-founder of a large hotel chain and a mutual fund in Boston. He also enjoyed the distinction of being a World War I aviator shot down in battle over France. Although he and my grandmother were just "Granny and Dadda" to me, I knew that they were considered by others to be exceptional people.

My grandfather, with his large bushy eyebrows and mustache, exerted an early influence on my ideas of what a man should be. Although quite taciturn, he exemplified calm stability and self-assurance to my youthful mind. Similarly, his selfless support for family and friends influenced my ideas of virtue and duty. He and my grandmother lived in an impressive modern home of perhaps 6,000 square feet on a hill in Concord, Massachusetts, the town where I was born and spent most of my life through eighth grade.

Perhaps because of the turmoil in my own immediate family, I equated the calm stability and competence of my grandfather with the wealth that seemed to be one of his personal attributes. My mother and father were deeply interested in spiritual search, but they were unable to ground their lives with material success.

In the early 1950s, they lived in India for two and a half years, where my father worked on a book entitled *Journeys On the Razor-Edged Path* about Eastern spirituality and studied with monks of the Ramakrishna Mission, and my mother learned hatha yoga.

But this and other ventures into the realm of the holy appeared to me to exhaust their resources and cause them to renounce mental and material stability. Despite my mother's financial resources and the opportunities presented to my father, they could not hold onto money or use it to bring peace and order into their lives and into the family. I viewed their scrimping as a sign of their inability to master life's challenges. I also did not understand why spiritual effort resulted in family turmoil. As a result, I concluded that wealth promoted peace to a greater extent than did spirituality.

The personal problems of my parents mounted, ultimately resulting in their divorce when I was eleven. My brother, sister, and I were dispersed to boarding schools when I was twelve.

In contrast, the wealth of my grandfather glued the extended family together. The trusts he established paid for the schooling of me, my brother, sister, and cousins through both prep schools and private colleges. The large oceanside summer estate that he reigned over on Cuttyhunk Island off the coast of Massachusetts provided my destination for many summers. It was a small kingdom in which he roamed as the undisputed lion.

I did not question whether or not it was truly proper for a family to husband to itself such resources. Although the ocean stretched before me, I did not search for a farther horizon than the interests of the family, for the stability of my grandfather's dominion filled me with hope for the future. Change seemed the only constant in my own life, as I moved frequently between boarding school dormitories and summer camps. Indeed, constancy seemed ambition enough to me at that age.

As I grew older the importance of wealth impressed itself more upon me. Because I was essentially apart from my family from the seventh grade onwards, self-reliance and personal control exercised a great appeal for me. It is true that I had no need to worry about money, but I still was not personally the master of its powers. Money promised the means to control my own destiny and even the destiny of others. I never thought it possible that I could have too much; indeed, money appeared to be the key to peace and freedom - a peace and freedom that only grew with the size of the treasure.

I visited my father in Atlanta after he and my mother were divorced. To make ends meet, he sold Fuller brushes in some of the more affluent neighborhoods. Although only twelve or so, I was not too young to realize that I was being used as a convenient tool to enhance sales. The pity of his situation contrasted sharply with the influence wielded by my grandparents. My grandfather was known and treated with the greatest respect when he entered a bank or auto dealership. I swelled with pride when accompanying him in the community and felt admiration for his accomplishments. In contrast, the hurt I felt with my father's financial situation carried over to a lack of respect for his spiritual ideals.

But by the time I was in my mid-teens, those very ideals began to exert a slow pull on me. I spent two summers during high school working in my mother's and second stepfather's metaphysical bookstore on the coast of Maine. That experience afforded me the opportunity to pore over numerous books on many spiritual subjects. I gained an appreciation there of the variety and wonder of the paths available to aspirants. And so, although I still related wealth to competency, I did not necessarily feel it to be the more important of the two. A tenuous balance had been struck. I knew that my own opportunity to prove myself financially would come in due time, but it could await the outcome of the spiritual quest.

By the time I reached college, I knew it was more important to seek understanding of life's meaning and goals than it was to find a profession that would make me wealthy. At Pomona College in California, I planned to study psychology. However, after a remarkable satori experience, in my freshman year, where I became spiritually awakened for a short time, I switched my major area of study to religion. Only then did I begin to truly value the spiritual tenets espoused by my parents. The power and magnificence of that illuminating event, revealed a new perspective on their aspirations. After meeting the curriculum prerequisites for a B.A. in religion, I concentrated mostly on Buddhism and Hinduism, which seemed to speak most clearly to what I had experienced.

And so a fundamental shift occurred. I had been deeply impressed for years by such Indian saints as Ramakrishna and Ramana Maharshi. Now I pursued that inclination, which had been fed by my mother's and father's interest in yoga and meditation, in which fields both were authors. With a growth in personal maturity and perhaps the ripening of ancient karma, I was at last able to see past the rubble of my parents' personal lives into the value of their aspirations, and I turned consciously onto the higher path.

Upon leaving college, I married a lovely young lady named Rose, whom I first met on a summer exchange program in Germany when I was fifteen. We had attended college on adjoining campuses in Claremont, California, and had shared a five-month semester-abroad program in Nepal in 1973. We moved to Tucson, Arizona, in 1975, where I landed a job as a stockbroker at Merrill Lynch.

I had acquired a great interest in the stock market in my college years, when I took classes in technical analysis in Los Angeles, but the job proved to be challenging for me because I was not sufficiently oriented to a sales profession. After almost two years at the brokerage firm, I switched into real estate sales. I benefitted financially on my own home from rapidly rising real estate values in Tucson, and I also bought three rental houses in 1978. Still, my cash flow was minimal and the money for purchasing the rentals came mostly from family members whom I enlisted as stockholders in a corporation I had created for that purpose.

The lure of making big money dimmed after several years spent in the effort. And so I again concentrated my attention on my spiritual search, recognizing that I finally had achieved the conditions that I had long sought to pursue my higher goals - a little time, money, and a place of my own. With some stability in my life, I chose to explore the path of Zen Buddhism. I had identified Zen as the most promising pursuit after the illuminating experience in my freshman year of college. In fact, the subject comprised the basis of my senior thesis. Still, by 1978 I was not satisfied with my progress. I had arrived at a wall that I was unable to find a way over or around. I recognized my own inability to penetrate to a higher understanding. Frustrated, I wondered what I could do to break the impasse. Thankfully, having reached the end of my own resources, I must have become eligible for divine grace.

At this time, I was introduced to Sathya Sai Baba by my mother, who, despite her maternal shortcomings in my own eyes, was considered by many to be a spiritual visionary. In fact, a best-selling book by Jess Stern entitled *Yoga, Youth, and Reincarnation* appeared in the early 1960s which portrayed her as something of a guru. She presented me with a copy of Murphet's book *Sai Baba Avatar* in October of 1978. That event initiated a whirlwind of spiritual activity for me. The discovery of the *avatar* put flame to the dry tinder in my heart. My mind raced and my heart leaped at the possibilities present in the discovery of God on earth. Every day I expected to awake and find that it was all just a dream, but the joy of that reality only grew deeper.

After reading the book, I cut a small picture of Sathya Sai Baba from its pages and placed it in a cheap plastic frame on my desk at home. Later I discovered that this picture portrayed Him shortly before He produced a Shiva lingam on the holy night of Shivaratri. At the time, I was impressed by the fact that the picture looked like the old black-and-white photos of Himalayan masters my mother kept on her altar. After a week or so, the picture produced small flecks of light gray ash, *vibhuti*, on its plastic covering. I was thrilled by this sign of patent divinity, but said nothing to Rose, although I later learned that she had also witnessed the appearance.

Shortly after this event, I decided to present the small black-and-white picture in a nicer manner, and so I carefully cleaned a new gold-colored frame. Being of a practical nature, I wiped the picture very clean, so that I would be sure to see any new manifestation of the light gray ash. I also ensured that the frame and glass were squeaky clean with Windex and paper towels. Sitting on the floor of my study, I leaned to my right to cut a piece of mat board. Turning back to the picture, which I had placed on the floor to my left, I noticed a small pile of vibhuti on the surface of the photo. When I lifted the photo to examine the grey substance, the ash rolled off the picture and into my hand. I was awed and shaken by this display of the presence of God. How could anyone explain such an act of grace? Why should the Divine One reward my small devotion with such a patent sign of His favor and omnipresence? How could I comprehend the marvelous love of God for His undeserving creature? I was overwhelmed by the implications of this small miracle.

When I told Rose of this phenomenon, she said somewhat facetiously: "That's very interesting. Perhaps we should go to see Baba in India - if He sends us a personal invitation." We had traveled through India for several weeks in the early 1970s after our semester in Nepal, but as "hippies" we had minimal physical comforts, which is perhaps why she was not eager to return there. And so she issued the challenge for direct evidence before committing to a return to the subcontinent.

We had heard of Sai Baba only weeks before. Who could reasonably expect that He would send us a "personal invitation" from the opposite side of the globe? It did not appear to be a realistic possibility. Surely the Lord of creation was not so easily placed at our beck and call. We were clearly no saints or great servants of the poor and downtrodden. Certainly He who rules the heavens and earth had better things to do than to call us into His presence. But, to our astonishment, within days something incredible happened.

A letter and travel flyer arrived in the mail from my mother. She wrote us that she planned to lead a group to India to see Sathya Sai Baba, although she had never been to visit Him before. In bold print at the top of the cover page were the words, "This is your personal invitation to visit Sathya Sai Baba in India."

We were amazed by this express granting of Rose's frivolous wish. Slowly and steadily, we became aware of the charming and captivating way of Sai. How sweetly and patiently He brought us along the path! What wonder and mystery He planted in our hearts!

But still we were deterred by the obstacles that such a trip presented. We knew travelling to India would be staggering for our budget. We were still in our mid-20s, and our minimal incomes precluded major new expenses. We had even considered renting out our home and living in an apartment to conserve money. Also, I felt that I could not easily abandon my job for the several weeks that would be required to complete such a journey. With a new home and no savings, we did not believe that the trip was a reasonable prospect.

However, within just a few weeks, events took a welcome turn. I quickly and easily sold a large piece of commercial real estate. The sale required little effort on my part. It almost happened by itself. My commission on the sale was more than $10,500. To top this "coincidence," my real estate broker terminated my employment at the same time. He explained that I was not putting enough effort into the job and that he wanted to end my complacency. This did not appear to be normal behavior for a broker directly following such a large sale. So, by January of 1979, within just two or three months of first hearing about Sathya Sai Baba, Rose and I winged our way to India for a six-week pilgrimage.

The circumstances of this incident began to show me that Sathya Sai Baba is the master of our destinies and that He also holds the strings of our purses. I began to learn that I was not the doer I had fancied myself to be: Swami is the one who plans all actions. Despite my own inability to produce income when required, He could fill my pockets from half a world away. As an interesting footnote, after having accomplished His goal of sending us on the trip, Swami repaired any unintended damage that was done. When we returned home, my real estate broker immediately offered me my job back.

Perhaps unconsciously, my attitudes about wealth began to change. Sathya Sai Baba does not sound the stern warnings about "gold" that Ramakrishna voiced, nor does He reflect the wary indifference of Ramana Maharshi. Baba teaches that money has its place in society, but must be used for the common good in recognition of our oneness. It should not accrue in massive quantities to a single individual or family, but should be used in a way that helps many.

> *Of course, a person must have enough to lead a simple life. But wealth accumulated beyond reasonable levels intoxicates the self and breeds evil desires and habits. Wealth has to be held in trust for activities that are beneficial, for promoting righteous living, and for fulfilling one's duties to society.*

Unfortunately, by late 1982, I still had not learned the lessons of financial contentment, nor had I apparently reduced my karmic monetary debts. I was working at Southwest Savings and Loan in Tucson as a branch manager of a small office. During the late fall, Swami engaged me in a *leela* (divine play) that was to reduce my financial ambitions and the size of my wallet. I had started trading stock index futures contracts for my own account, an outgrowth of my previous market charting and later employment at Merrill Lynch. The trading system that I learned in Los Angeles formed the basis of what I believed to be a successful market strategy. I had continued to follow the stock market, and I now believed that I could profit handsomely from the fluctuations of the stock indexes.

Over the period of two or three months in late 1982, I pulled in over $5,000 in my spare time with very little effort, trading mostly stock index futures, which were new at the time. The funding for this activity was made possible by an inheritance I had just received as a result of my mother's untimely demise. Because of my successes in the market, I resolved to carry on my trading activity as a full-time vocation, feeling that more attention to the matter could only brighten the prospects for success.

Well, upon deciding to leave my job at the bank, Rose and I again traveled to India for our first visit with Baba since 1979. On this second trip in January of 1983, Swami granted us an interview, and during it He questioned those in the room about their work. Unsolicited by any question from me, Swami indicated to me that I worried too much about the market's fluctuations. He said, "Up and down, up and down, do not worry. I will bless." `

"Well," I thought, "Now I have it made. Swami will bless my trading and things will work out great!" I had not even mentioned the subject and Swami had offered His blessings! I prepared myself mentally to live the lifestyle of a rich and carefree futures trader. It was not a difficult task. I felt that great monetary success was sure to follow and that it would naturally grant me inner peace and contentment. Like my grandfather, I would be a lion among men. I could engage in generous philanthropy and use my time to support spiritual activities. My troubles were over! I too could amass a fortune and receive the veneration of my family and society! Wealth would surely squelch any previous lack of peace and contentment that I had felt! I was on cloud nine.

However, it was not to be as I had expected. When I returned from India and got down to the business of trading, I could do almost nothing right for the next 10 months. I amassed only large trading losses. Naturally, I kept waiting for my fortune to change, having received Swami's blessing and the injunction not to worry. I was sure that the losses were only a test of my faith and fortitude. But clearly, I knew neither the real nature of Swami's blessing nor the type of labor that Swami really expected of me. Sathya Sai Baba encourages us to engage in productive labor. He does not encourage us to amass money beyond our own just needs.

> *The sruthis (scriptures) direct that man has to earn just enough for his upkeep by honest means and use the rest of his time and skill for the general good.*

When I was ready to throw in the towel and accept my losses, I had a dream which took place in a hospital setting. I was performing a ceremonial worship to Baba when I saw ugly strips of a waste-like material, which I understood to be karma, that I had piled in a heap on the floor. I walked from the room and the building aware that I had shed a harmful karmic burden through the experience of financial loss and now was free of the burden. Indeed, Swami had blessed me with this spiritual benefit, but not with the material gains I had expected or desired. And so the purpose of His play became clear. He enabled me to progress spiritually by causing me to lose monetarily. Surely also His injunction not to worry had been well said, for none of my worrying made any difference to the outcome. Worry had only made me unhappy, with no concurrent benefit.

Again, I learned that I am not the doer. Clearly my experience with market losses was arranged for a purpose. It had nothing to do with my own competency in financial affairs or lack of the same. The divine play helped me learn some humility and showed me the fickleness of loss and gain, for loss and gain were demonstrated to be subservient to divine will. My loss was not a result of my own inability any more than my gain had resulted from personal skill.

My sense of the unreality of this loss was heightened when Swami again repaired the unintended damage from His play. I again found myself without a job. I attributed the loss of my employment to Swami's leela and appealed to his sense of fairness to make amends. Within a week or so of my appeal, I not only reacquired my old position at the bank, but I returned with a promotion to manage a larger office. In addition, my original hire date, four years previous, was reinstated, along with all of my sick time - amounting to some six weeks worth. My original hire date was also credited toward my pension accrual. A nice final touch was my assignment to branch number 45 on November 9th. (Nine is the divine number and Swami's number).

This experience taught me sympathy for those who incur loss due to divine plans. Like the heros and villains of ancient Greek plays, I also was a plaything of the gods. I began to see that error in judgment was not the only reason for loss, any more than monetary gain necessarily indicated personal or spiritual competence. Perhaps the lesson also softened my heart to the events which made my mother's and father's lives so difficult. It showed me that one may not be given the luxury of ideal material conditions while trying to establish peace within. I started to believe that good actions and pure thoughts are a greater and safer form of wealth than coins and currency, which are so easily subject to loss and gain. For surely the events of our lives are not entirely under our own control. Perhaps our only prerogative is how we react to those events.

*While you should develop this saving habit here for the sake of old age and a rainy day, it is necessary that you should develop the 'saving habit' for the hereafter, so that you may be saved.... Dharma (righteousness) and sathya (truth) and prema (love) are the currency accepted by that other bank.*

Sathya Sai Baba says, "My life is my message." It was a message I took to heart. His example dispelled my earlier notions of money as a magic key to peace and satisfaction. Sai Baba is a model of virtue, and yet He holds no personal possessions or trappings of wealth. He wears simple clothes, lives frugally, and acts only for others. Although He wields great influence and power, money does not adhere to him. His example expresses great selflessness, for He uses money only for the benefit of others. Such wisdom should guide the control of wealth so that it will benefit many. High ideals of behavior and wide horizons of community should guide our own use of money.

*Wealth without wisdom becomes an instrument of exploitation and tyranny; wisdom without wealth becomes mere fantasy and a bundle of blueprints. Use makes them worthwhile; misuse makes them disastrous.*

Since the futures trading episode, I have experienced many gains and losses. They do not hold the same importance in how I evaluate myself that they once did. I am convinced that I will receive whatever is my due, for better or for worse, by the will of Sathya Sai Baba. He places us in situations where we win or lose so that we can learn that which He wants to teach us. The gain or loss is given by Him for our own ultimate good.

Sai's teachings have given me a new perspective. By freeing me from the notion that money conveys peace, I am better able to focus on the true sources of contentment. Concern for the needs of others and surrender to divine will are more genuine sources of comfort than coins and currency. In the workplace, when I place the final gain or loss in the hands of God, I see that many people benefit. The expression of real caring in the office or shop eliminates common antagonisms between employees, customers, and management. I see that it is not necessary for me to promote any particular philosophy to any of these groups. The natural consideration for others that develops when we surrender to God creates bonds of true affection between workers and customers. Such attitudes do more for business than sales goals and five-year plans.

As a bank branch manager, I was able to test the concept of nonattachment in practice. By my expressing true concern for workers and customers, a feeling of caring and happiness spread to everyone in the office. The result caused employees to describe the atmosphere of the office as "magical." Customers often commented on the family-like atmosphere of the branch. For when we surrender the results to the Lord, we can concentrate on doing our duty to the best of our ability, while remembering what is really important in our lives.

The savings association at which I worked for twelve years was sold to a very large bank, which in turn was soon merged into an even larger bank. The process of closing the branch where I worked elicited numerous heartfelt solicitations for the welfare of all the employees. The genuine outpouring of concern from customers dispelled any notion I might have had that the joy I had in coming to work was a result of my wearing "rose-colored glasses." My own inner transformation enabled me to find joy in my business relationships, but it had also translated into an atmosphere in the office that was clear to all but the most casual observer. And despite the arrival and departures of many employees over the years, the feeling persisted and was apparent enough to be remarked upon by many.

I am not sure if it is possible to create a similar atmosphere in a large bank. The demands of ever greater economic efficiency squeeze out the time spent on human relationships. Perhaps it is too early to say, but the worldwide rush towards greater competition and the fierce fight for profit threatens all but the strongest competitors in the marketplace. When personal and corporate profit are held in higher esteem than the common good, the very structure of society is threatened. I hope that the future holds a place for benevolence in the workplace. I must believe that it does, for a spiritual realization of the oneness of all people is essential for our spiritual health. I hope that such ideals will prompt the strong to moderate their desire for monetary gain at the expense of the weak. In the rush toward higher productivity, employment of the uneducated and jobless should also receive consideration. I believe that

Sathya Sai Baba will show us the way.

*Everyone should respect all others as one's own kin, having the same divine spark and the same divine nature. Then there will be effective production, economic consumption, and equitable distribution, resulting in peace and the promotion of love. Now, love based on the innate divinity is absent, and so there is exploitation and deceit, greed and cruelty.*

And so I have come full circle. At one time the acquisition of money seemed the key to peace and mastery. Now I believe that moderating my desire for personal gain offers the best opportunity for my happiness. When I moderate my own desires, I have more to give to others. The satisfaction of caring for others outweighs the happiness of stashing a hoard of gold and silver. I do not believe that life holds great happiness to the one who hoards wealth. That hoarding turns into fear of loss and avarice for gain. When I give to others, I believe that I nurture my inner divinity while also gaining the higher joy of serving them. Wealth is best employed to promote the health, education, and welfare of all. When we give of ourselves and believe in our common divine destiny with all others, life becomes truly joyful and worthwhile.

# JOURNEY INTO THE TRUTH
Renate M. Kuchardt

My search to find truth began in 1969 when I attended a lecture by Maharishi Mahesh Yogi at the University in Berlin.

I was fascinated by this man's calmness, tranquility and self-control while he was being questioned and counterattacked by many students who believed themselves to be so much smarter than any other generation or person present in the auditorium. I left the lecture with the desire to learn yoga and to be like him.

I was a nervous child. Food represented pleasure and comfort to me, and I was always eating too much. My thoughts and ideas always ran quickly, and I talked too fast; often I was asked to repeat myself and to speak more slowly. I suffered from acne and had little self-confidence. In elementary school, classmates picked on me all the time. I was quite unhappy growing up, and given the political situation in Berlin in the sixties, I was fearful most of the time. I also agonized over the separation from part of my family when the Berlin Wall was erected. Out of this pain came feelings of hatred toward the East German and Soviet Union regimes and, consequently, because of all the injustice I saw around me, I became interested in politics. I turned into an anti-Vietnam war protestor. However, I always believed in God and often prayed to him. My parents always reminded me to speak the truth and not to hurt anyone. I felt truly guilty if I lied when I did foolish things like missing a day in school.

I was determined to change and in college decided that yoga would be my path. I bought a book on yoga and started meditation and physical yoga exercises. The book I used was written by Indra Devi. Many years later, when I was living in the United States, I found out that she was devoted to Sai Baba.

The book contained helpful breathing techniques, *asanas*

(yoga postures), meditations, vegetarian diet suggestions, and instruction on *dharmic* behavior, which I immediately tried to put into practice.

Dharmic life to me means no killing, lying, stealing, hurting, adultery, or gossip: basically to live according to the Ten Commandments. We all have good intentions, but to speak the truth can sometimes be painful and uncomfortable. In business it may jeopardize one's reputation or position.

Baba has helped me endure the daily obstacles of life in a world where most people only know how to worship materialism and therefore put material things before God. God often is forgotten and only remembered when calamity interrupts their lives. We devotees are lucky to have the best role model there is, Sri Sathya Sai Baba, to help us with our struggle with dharma.

Dharma comes in all forms, shapes and sizes. Whether we are young or old, whether we want it or not, it does not matter. We have to learn to be conscious of it. It takes strength, love, and will power. If I had listened to my inner voice, I would not have had to endure so many difficult situations. Each moment of truth counts because tomorrow we may not be alive to rectify the wrongs we have done.

Early on in my career, in 1973, I worked in Berlin for a publication company as an executive secretary. My supervisor had an accident and passed away. I was then transferred to the most difficult working situation I could imagine. The new department consisted of ten employees who were under the supervision of a recovering alcoholic who had started drinking again. This turned her into a monster. When she was drinking an enormous amount of hard liquor and wine throughout the day, she gave instructions she could not remember the next day. She would then rage at us when she saw the work we had done, which she "did not want."

Our team worked very well together and we liked our work, which involved selecting pictures for books or other publications that could be of importance or part of history. Since I worked very closely with our supervisor, I made an effort to soften the problems she created with other co-workers. However, her drinking increased and she lost control of all her emotions, throwing tantrums most of the time. At this point, I knew I had to do something. I felt disgust and disrespect for the woman and, out of this feeling, I mailed her an anonymous letter containing information on Alcoholics Anonymous. On the one hand, I hoped she would get help and improve, but I admit, I also wanted to annoy her with this letter. At the same time, I was terrified that she would find out who had sent it.

I finally filed a complaint with the worker's committee, although I risked being identified and going through additional hell with her. On the way to the committee meeting, my heart started palpitating and my hands got cold. Although the committee sympathized with me, there was not enough evidence to fire her. They were aware of the problem, but could only act if she did something drastically wrong.

I realized the situation was hopeless, so I decided to leave the job. After I gave my notice, however, I had six more weeks to work with her, and it became an almost unbearable situation. I thought, "How is it that a single person has so much power to mistreat and destroy human beings and get away with it?" That's what I believed then, but it turned out differently. Many years later, I found out that she was demoted and had to work among the employees she had treated so badly. I have learned a great deal from this: no one, except our Creator, has power over us unless we let them. To do the right thing is essential, even if it means being very uncomfortable.

My next venture in the business world was as the assistant to the owner of a clothing manufacturing company. I respected him for his kindness toward his employees. Especially after the preceding experience, it was nice to work for a humane person. I was the only bilingual employee and worked as a translator and, later on, headed the claims department. My supervisor did not speak English, which probably was the turning point in this situation. He saw me as an equal, even though I had no idea of dressmaking terminology or details. I had a good working relationship with him and never any problems, and he appreciated my work. I was thankful for this job; it was a nice environment to work in - and heaven on earth compared to the previous job!

Then one day I became very upset when I found out that he had tapped into the telephone line of one of his employees. Right in front of me, he would tap into her conversation to see how often she was making private calls. The situation made me nervous and tense because it looked like I was collaborating with him and because I would not want to have anybody listening into my calls, whether business or private. This became a real issue for me. He was listening for a long time, and he was violating her privacy. It was clear he wanted to collect enough evidence to fire her. Apparently he did not want to give her a second chance.

Remembering my previous job, I did not want to risk losing my good working relationship with him. I was afraid to address the issue and wasn't sure it was my place to do so. And he was the owner of the business, not just a supervisor. I even considered warning the employee, but was afraid she would say or do something that would put my position in jeopardy and that I would no longer be trusted.

Every day, seeing this woman being watched by him made me feel like I was the eavesdropper myself. It was horrible looking into her eyes and knowing what was going on. However, I see now that I did not want to tell her what was going on because I did not want to jeopardize my position. I could have saved myself a lot of stress if I had either left the room or expressed my feelings about what was going on.

Later, another supervisor, at a different place, approached me to spy for him in order to find grounds to fire two people he did not like. When he made the "offer" to me, I was speechless, embarrassed, and humiliated: how could this be happening to me again? I told my supervisor, "I do not know how to help you. To my knowledge, these two employees do good work." I wondered if he would then treat me differently or if I would continue to have a future with the company. Yet I knew I never would have a peaceful moment at work if I agreed to participate in a scheme like this. Luckily the problem was quickly solved by that supervisor being transferred to another location.

Both these cases happened in the beginning of my career. I was too young and too inexperienced to really know how to handle these situations.

In August 1988, I made my first trip to India to see Sri Sathya Sai Baba. I was not a devotee yet, but I was very eager to see Him after watching Him 18 years earlier on German television. However, before I arrived Baba had broken His hip and therefore He did not make any appearances. He only came out to give *darshan* and a discourse for Krishna's birthday. I was lucky to get a front-row seat for this celebration, which made it possible to see and experience Him very closely. For two hours I watched Him give a discourse **standing** - with a broken hip. This left me absolutely astonished. No words can describe what I felt for him. I knew than that He was to become my path. I left the ashram as a devotee and with the desire to see Him in His full glory.

Many trips to India followed. In 1991, on one of these visits, I had a real dharmic dilemma. Without even thinking, I purchased a ring and paid for it with U.S. dollars. I did not know at that time it was illegal to pay for an item with foreign currency. I knew we should not exchange money on the black market, but to go in a store and pay with foreign currency did not seem wrong to me. However, the next day I attended a lecture at the ashram where it was stressed we were not to pay with foreign currency but only with rupees, traveller's checks, or in some other legal manner. It was brought to our attention that violators, if caught, would be arrested and the consequences could be devastating. I wanted not only to do the right thing but especially to abide by the rules of the ashram. In my mind,

I saw myself being thrown out of the country, never able to come back to see Baba. This warning got completely into my bones and I thought I would always remember it.

During a trip to Baba a few months ago, I made some purchases from a vendor I trusted. He was so nice, and I never dreamed in my wildest imagination that a sweet person like this could be devious. It was around Christmas time, and I was looking for gifts to take home. I got attached to a very pretty ring, something I had always wanted. The vendor must have sensed my desire for it and immediately made me a discount offer - if I would pay him in dollars. My first instinct was to say, "No, you cannot do this, this is not legal and Baba would not approve of it." I thought to myself, "Maybe I shouldn't buy this ring at all." But in the end, it was not the temptation of getting the ring for less money but rather the inconvenience of going to the bank again that made me act dishonorably and agree to his offer. While the transaction was going on, I felt very uncomfortable and knew I should not pay in dollars. Nevertheless, once the transaction was irreversible, I started to justify my wrongdoing by thinking, "This is the last time I will ever do this."

I went back for a second purchase, but this time with a credit card. I purchased a silver bracelet and negotiated a price of 900 rupees. Proud and determined not to be lured again into an illegal and dishonest action, I handed the vendor my credit card and the purchase was made. During my travel through India and Germany, I made a lot of credit card charges. When I came home I found an error on my credit card bill, namely 1,900 rupees for the bracelet, 1,000 rupees more than I had signed for. After investigating, the credit card company denied my objection to the dispute since I could not produce my charge slip. Of all the charges I made, the **only slip missing** was the one from this transaction. The copy they sent from India, the merchant's copy, clearly showed the manipulation of the amount to read 1,000 rupees more. Soon after, in New York, I went to get the stone reset in the first ring that I had bought with dollars, and I also learned that it was a piece of junk.

I was terribly disappointed in myself. In the middle of the Abode of Peace, so very close to Sai Baba, I had been greedy, selfish, and dishonest. I had not listened to my inner voice. I knew it was wrong while I was making the purchase, yet I could not bring myself to be stronger in that moment and overcome the temptation.

To me this has been a valuable lesson in instant karma. I have been immediately punished, and I welcome it. Karmic consequences can be severe but, I must admit, I got off the hook easily in order to learn this lesson.

I have learned that there is no way to be a little bit dharmic: it has to be lived all the way. A good reminder for me is the saying, "There is no way to be a little bit pregnant." This is funny but true and can easily be remembered.

I believe to overcome a major situation is sometimes easier than the little daily trials which we believe don't have much importance. For instance, what about "white lies"? Is taking pens and paper home from business stealing? Is using the office postage meter for private mail stealing? I believe it is.

I have had my problems with this when everybody at work puts their mail through the postage meter and then encourages me to use it, too. It is not the money that makes it tempting, but the time spent going to the post office when there is no time to be found. Usually, I am alone. Nine out of ten people go in one direction and I go in the other. It is a challenge, but this is when it counts to stay on the right path.

How do you deal with a situation where you see someone doing something dishonest? What is our obligation? Is it wrong not to interfere, not to speak the truth, to knowingly be passive? What if somebody lies or steals and I am a witness to it? Am I obliged to speak up even if I am not a part of the situation? I have not found the answers to these questions. I believe each situation has to be considered individually.

What about gossip that can hurt someone, gossip we have

taken part in? Here is some priceless instruction from Baba: *"Don't speak unless you can improve upon silence."*

By birthright, human beings are all equal. Nobody is higher or lower, superior or inferior - at least, it should be this way. Believing in this has helped me to speak up for important issues, whether it be at work, home or any place. This feels good and liberating. The key is to present it nicely, without fear or excitement. When I listen to my inner voice, I do not have any problem at all. From all these experiences, I have learned to be more truthful.

> *Dharma is the road for individual and social progress, in this world and through this world to the next. It is eternal, basic, fundamental. The principles may not be altered or adjusted to suit personal whims or pressing problems that appear formidable to the eyes of some individuals or group of persons. It is like the mother who has to be accepted, not like the wife whom you can choose or discard.*

Presently, I am working in international trade. Often my job is to organize the trade shows for our company. I am now blessed with a supervisor who makes a difference himself: his picture should be in the dictionary for the word dharma. It is a true pleasure to work for him. He does everything right, and he is an extremely pleasant, cheerful, righteous human being who cares about all people. He knows that I am a Sai Baba devotee, and when I become stressed, he often reminds me who I am. This seems like a miracle to me after all the experiences I have had in the past. Perhaps I have learned something after all these years and all these challenges.

Dharmic behavior now comes more naturally to me, and it is becoming more of a habit. Of course, I still have my struggles, daily trials, and tribulation, and sometimes my mind wants to persuade me to go in the wrong direction. Most of the time, my will power succeeds and the right action prevails. It makes me feel good, happy, and grateful - grateful, because no bad karma is created. Hopefully, good karma will manifest and will serve as a balance for any dishonest or unethical behavior that I created in the past. Dharmic behavior is very rewarding and contagious. It goes beyond ourselves. Dharma can change the world and one day bring peace to all mankind.

> *If there is righteousness in the heart,*
> *There will be beauty in character.*
> *If there is beauty in character,*
> *There will be harmony in the home.*
> *Where there is harmony in the home,*
> *There will be order in the nation.*
> *When there is order in the nation,*
> *There will be peace in the world.*

*"Whatever is done in an attitude of dedication and surrender is a component of the Dharma which leads to Realization."*

Sathya Sai Baba

# THROUGH DHARMIC DILEMMAS
Lt. Gen. (Retd.) M.L. Chibber, Ph.D.,
Dr. (Mrs.) R. Chibber

*Let every human being remake himself. Let us understand that we live not for money-making, not for fulfilling our wants, not for scholarly and intellectual talents, but for spiritual development.*

It was a dharmic dilemma that brought us to Sai Baba in 1979. The dilemma, perhaps, was just an excuse. The time had come for us to be eligible to receive His direct guidance in understanding the purpose of human birth. I realized this when I once grumbled to Swami in 1989 about the fact that I had been in Bangalore in 1945-46 at the Army Officers Training School. We complained, "Swami, why did you not let us come to you then?" With a twinkle in His eyes, all He said was, "Yes, yes, I used to see you from a distance!"

We have been spiritually inclined since our childhood. We inherited this tendency from our parents. After Rameshi and I were married and had children, we would spend our leave trekking to places like Amarnath, Gangotri, Badrinath, and Rishikesh in the Himalayas. We also visited shrines of all the faiths of India. We went to virtually all the learned gurus in the country. We did derive much benefit. Our faith in the power called God, symbolized by Lord Shiva, was reinforced. But there was something lacking.

When we look back on the decades until 1979, when Baba finally called us, we find that whenever we prayed ardently to Lord Shiva, we invariably got whatever we asked for. But then our prayers were for mundane worldly things. I now understand why Swami did not create the opportunity for me to go to him in 1945-46, or for that matter in 1974 when he visited Amristar and I was commanding the Army Division there. Obviously we were not yet ready for the spiritual education Swami imparts.

In 1979, I was promoted to the rank of Lieutenant General and placed in command of the country's counter-offensive force. It is a most satisfying job for a professional soldier to lead a force of 200,000 men and all the military hardware needed for a rapid and effective counter-strike in case India was attacked.

Knowing our interest in spiritual matters, a staff officer in my headquarters gave me a copy of Howard Murphet's book *Sai Baba, Man of Miracles*. My wife also got another book from her brother. When we look back, we realize that our time to come to Swami had finally arrived. We faced two dilemmas, two acts written by the Author in the drama we call life.

The first was related to improving leadership in my counter-offensive force. This triggered research. Fifteen years of long quest, trials, and experimentation culminated in a book I wrote entitled *Sai Baba's Mahavakya on Leadership*.[1] When Baba wrote the Foreword and the Afterword for the book, I realized the working of His guiding hand through those fifteen years of endeavor. This first dilemma was based on my ignorance that I (the versatile commander!) could "fix" the problem of improving leadership. Not knowing that effective leadership is a byproduct of spiritual growth, I felt at a loss when faced with the marginal results of my efforts in this field. I did not know whether to give up the effort or to continue. The puppeteer (Swami) anonymously made me continue.

The second dilemma related to my being appointed to a high-powered committee to revise the parameters for higher command in the Indian Army. It is this second problem which

---

[1] Published by *Leela Press, Inc.*, Faber, VA.

developed into a serious dharmic dilemma.[2]

A person has his dharma as a human being, a son, a mother, a father, a brother, a sister, a spouse, a worker, a friend, a leader, a citizen, and so on. Dharma implies that a person has only duties and obligations. As Swami so often explains, rights flow out automatically from one's dharma well-performed. There are absolutely *no* rights divorced from duties and obligations in the Indian spiritual and cultural heritage. The words of Swami on this score are categorical and unambiguous:

> *Authority and influence have to emerge from the discharge of one's duties. Then only will they be effective. We must be convinced that rights are deserved only by the discharge of obligations.*

The dilemma arose from the unwritten purpose of the committee to which I had been appointed. It was informally conveyed to us that we were to dilute the very stringent standards laid down for selection for higher command appointments in the Army. There was clamor from the officers in the Army to make it easy, and the then-hierarchy of the Army was merely responding to this demand. To give respectability to this step, a committee of five professionals with good reputation had been appointed.

The history of war has repeatedly taught a lesson: If you dilute your higher command, you build a disaster in war. However, Army hierarchies repeatedly succumb to pressures and erode the parameters, which should stay inflexible. Dilution normally occurs during long spells of peace.

When the committee met, it was clear that three members

---

[2]The best explanation of dharma for me was by a Polish lady journalist, Taya Zinkin. After working in India for a few decades she built the meaning of dharma into her description of a true gentleman, a *sthithprajnya* (a person of steady wisdom as described in the *Bhagavad Gita*). To practice dharma is to "have a sense of duties and obligations of one's position whatever it may be."

were fully in tune with the unwritten purpose of the committee. One was silent. I expressed my reservations against the dilution but agreed to examine the statistics and other inputs that had a bearing on the problem. In a series of meetings, a vast plethora of figures was presented by whiz-kids. Listening to the statistical acrobatics, I recalled my eminent professor of mathematics in college. He started the class on statistics by a quip, "There are lies, damned lies, and there are statistics!" By the sixth meeting, the member who was acting as secretary had prepared the draft report. Its conclusion was that the committee unanimously recommended all the dilution measures that the Army hierarchy desired. I flatly said that it was not possible for me to sign a report that in the long run could result in a setback in war. I explained to them the recent British experience between World War I and World War II. The British had diluted their criteria and the result was that "intelligent, hardworking, and pliable officers" forged ahead. Most of the battle disasters in the first two years of World War II that the British suffered were largely due to this fact. Intelligent but pliable officers, unfortunately, do not win battles; character invariably beats cleverness. The meeting was adjourned.

After a few days, it was discreetly conveyed to me that either I sign the report or else it would be the end of my military career. Here was a first-rate dilemma: In the remaining six years of my service I could most certainly rise up to be Commander-in-Chief of one of the regional armies in India; or I could be ignominiously vanquished. The dilemma was extremely distressing. Should I choose what is best for my career or should I perform my dharma?

About seventeen years earlier, I had faced a similar situation when I was a major. The then-Chief of General Staff of the Army got extremely upset with something I had recommended. Reading between the lines of my note, he felt I was casting aspersions on his courage. I was marched up before him. He fretted and fumed and ended his ranting with the words, "I will have you thrown out of the Army!" I was a bit surprised that he should perceive a meaning that I had not at all intended. I had just returned from a year's training at the Staff College in England and was on the fast track for advancement in the Army, and now I was on the brink of being terminated for something very trivial. I was certainly worried. So I went home and shared the problem with my wife. She was a pillar of strength. She is a medical doctor and she said, "Don't worry, I will set up a medical clinic and if you help me, we will have a roaring practice." Then she added with some amusement, "Even though I know fully well that you will do the roaring and I will do the practice!" Fortunately some well-wishers intervened to explain the truth to the Chief of General Staff and the storm blew over. So I knew my wife would be with me when I faced this new dharmic dilemma.

It was at this time that Swami came into our lives in a big way. Reading Howard Murphet's book was a great eye-opener. Then, with the help of the *Sai Samithi*, my staff officer assisted my wife in arranging a bhajan in the Army House. The vibrations, the disciplined precision, and the love pouring out of Sai brothers and sisters who helped in this bhajan conveyed to us that we had, at last, found the way home.

The dilemma I was facing became a small routine problem. I wrote out a well-argued and strong dissenting note for the report and sent it off to Army Headquarters. A sense of great relief and joy for having done my dharma engulfed me. I forgot all about the problem and got busy training my force.

Then things started happening. We felt Swami's instant help in various mundane problems. But the biggest surprise was that I was selected to become the Adjutant General of the Indian Army. I instinctively knew the divine hand was in this development.

Within two weeks of taking over this crucial appointment, and at my wife's determined insistence, we flew down to Bangalore and drove to Prasanthi Nilayam for Swami's darshan. This was our first, and a most elevating, visit to

Swami. The impact that the *sarva dharma* logo carved on Swami's door made on me culminated in the establishment of the Army Institute of National Integration, which offers training programs to familiarize Army officials with the rudimentary teachings of all faiths. The Institute is helping enormously in a multi-religious, multi-ethnic, and multi-lingual country. Lots of wars have been fought in the world due to ignorance of this inherent harmony. It took four years to get this implemented, but whatever Swami inspires, eventually succeeds.

Swami also granted us an interview. He materialized a medallion and asked me to always keep it with me: "It will protect you." Only after a few years did I fully comprehend the meaning of this simple sentence spoken so casually.

As the Commander-in-Chief of India's Northern Command, I had a fairly hectic three years of no-war-no-peace involvement in various small and big local operations and battles. After retiring from the Army, we once again visited Swami. I had already picked up from the market a stainless steel ring with Swami's portrait on it. During an interview He noticed the ring and asked, "Where did you get this ring from?" I replied that I had bought it in the market. He told me to take it off, and it was passed around to all the devotees. When it finally reached Baba, He blew on it, and it became a beautiful silver ring which He put on my finger. At this moment, my wife intervened. She was sitting very close to Baba. She said, "Swami, you are very partial to men. A few years back you gave him a medallion and now you have given him a ring. I am the one who brought him to you and you have given me nothing." Having said this, she took off her simple marriage ring and held it out to Baba. He smiled and said, "Wait, wait."

Later, when we went to the inner interview room, Baba was oozing with love. Placing His hand on my wife's head like a loving father, He said, "I have already made you a *sumangali*, what more do you want?" She understood, but I did not have the slightest idea what the Sanskrit word sumangali meant.

That evening while waiting in the darshan line, I asked some of the older devotees the meaning of the word and told them the story of the interview. They were amused at my ignorance and explained to me, "Swami must have postponed your 'going up' to prevent your wife from becoming a widow." It was then that numerous incidents during operations when I could have been blown to pieces flashed across my mind. I remembered how He had given me the silver medallion with such a casual remark, "It will protect you."

Two day later, much to the joy of my wife, Swami materialized diamond earrings for her. While Swami was putting them in her ears, she quipped, "Swami, this Army guy never gave me any diamonds!" To this, Swami replied, "You must understand the meaning of diamond. It means die-mind." Then with a mischievous twinkle in His eyes, He looked at me and inquired, "Are you feeling jealous because I have given diamonds to your wife and only silver to you?" I said I was quite happy with whatever He gave me. "No, no, give your ring." After the ring was passed around among the devotees, He blew on it and it became gold with His beautiful portrait. Later, in the private interview room, He asked me with some concern if I would rather have stones in the ring instead of the portrait. Of course I was more than happy with what I already had.

Swami gives us this demonstration of converting energy into matter (like *vibhuti* and trinkets) and on occasions, reconverting matter back into energy, for a purpose. It is to help us understand that He and we are all divine. Once this understanding dawns on us and we move toward experiencing our reality, then we do not have to make an effort to live a dharmic life; it will come naturally to us.

His therapy is different for each one of us. It is based on the balance sheet of *karma* and on the level to which each one of us has evolved. But the goal of the therapy is the same for all of us: to understand our reality and then help us experience it, to help us grow and be what we really are - divine. Swami has very clearly explained it:

*Transmuting "man" into "God" and experiencing that ananda and bliss is the one and only achievement for which life is to be devoted.*

It was almost ten years after we came to Him that He decided to give me the major dose of spiritual therapy. He called us for an interview. It was the usual group of about 25 people. After distributing vibhuti to the ladies, He sat down on His chair. Then He looked me straight in the eyes and said, "Spirituality is very easy. All you have to do is to understand and then experience that 'I am I.'" I nearly hit the roof. He made it sound so simple, whereas saints and sages have spent lifetimes in penance. I was also foggy about the real meaning of "I am I." Then He want on to explain, "If you think you are Ramaya or Ratan Lal or Chibber, then you are deluded." Every act of Swami has a deep meaning. When He gives a therapy, He also arranges for help. Slowly, step by step, we were helped during the next few years to comprehend the deeper meaning of "I am I." Swami in His various incarnations had tried to teach this fundamental truth to mankind: all that we perceive is the temporary projection of the one formless reality which is omnipresent, omnipotent, and omniscient. It is this truth that has been articulated thus:

*I am that I am* is the Biblical articulation;
*I and my Father are one,* said Jesus;
*Ik Onkar (All is One),* said Guru Nanak;
*Annal Haq (I am the Truth),* articulated a Muslim Saint,
   Mansur Al Hajj of Baghdad;
*So Ham (I am That),* the Perennial Philosophy; in Sanskrit
   termed the Sanathana Dharma.

Even today, with information technology at its height, we are still having difficulty comprehending this basic truth. Without this basic understanding, our attempts to live a dharmic life become a struggle at best or a mere slogan at worst.

I recall an interview with Swami which we had the good fortune of having with Dr. John Hislop[3] and his wife. Swami was, as usual, in His expansive and loving mood. He asked John if he was facing any problems in America. "Yes, Swami, how to satisfy devotees who want proof that you are God." Swami looked at John for a moment and said, "I am love; tell them that." He had summarized His famous advice:

*Duty without love is deplorable. Duty with love is desirable. Love without duty is Divine. Duty implies force or compulsion while love is spontaneous and expresses itself without external promptings.*

There is, however, a linked problem. It is difficult enough to believe that Swami is God, but the truth that we are also God is incomprehensible to many of us. Yet Swami repeatedly tells us that not only *He*, but each one of us is divine. There are numerous devotees who are highly evolved and understand this truth and live their lives the way divine life should be lived. But there are also a large number, like me, who are a bit foggy about all these higher philosophical assertions. It is for this reason that in almost every discourse by Swami, He emphasizes that everything is a form of God; that everyone is divine; that all is one. In spite of all of this, the main spiritual questions that aspirants ask are directly or indirectly related to this fundamental truth. Repeatedly these questions come up for discussion during the daily lectures that are organized for devotees at Prasanthi Nilayam and Brindavan.

---

[3] Dr. Hislop is the author of *Conversations with Sathya Sai Baba* and *My Baba and I*. At that time, he was head of the Sai Organization in the United States.

When we carefully read Swami's discourses, we notice that, again and again, He makes three declarations to drive home this fundamental truth. In fact, He very often reiterates these declarations even during interviews.

The first declaration is "I am always with you. I am all around you. I am on your right, on your left, in front of you, behind you, above you and below you." Many people understand the import of this declaration, but then there are others who start wondering: Swami certainly has a very extensive aura and what He says would be true when we are in Prasanthi or Brindavan, but how is it possible when we go back to Delhi, New York, Tokyo or Rio? The doubt lingers on.

The second declaration He makes is "you are in Me and I am in you." Again, to many of us this assertion causes confusion. We wonder, how can this be possible? I remember an incident in April 1993 in Kodaikanal. That year was a time for the overseas devotees. Almost every single day, Swami gave a discourse, and He had instructed that priority should be given to overseas devotees for entering into the small hall. A tall American became friendly with me. We would discuss spirituality, dharma, ethics while waiting long hours on the darshan lines. One day, Swami repeated this declaration. When we were leaving after the discourse, this American tapped me on the shoulder and said, "General, I don't get this. How on earth could I be in Swami and He in me? I am seven feet tall and Swami is just over five." All I could say was, "Oh, Ted, he was talking spiritually." But what was the spiritual message in this declaration? I had no crystal clear comprehension.

The third declaration he makes causes the maximum confusion in the minds of many of us. He looks you straight in the eye and, pointing with His index finger, articulates slowly and very, very deliberately, "You are God. I am God, so are you. We are one." I spent a good deal of my adult life looking for God in the form of Shiva in the Himalayan peaks and shrines. Many of us imagine God sitting somewhere up in heaven with His supercomputer, punching in every good or bad deed of ours. Then He eventually decides if we will go to heaven or burn in hell. And here is Swami telling us, "You are God." It shatters all our paradigms.

Swami, in His compassion, asked my wife and me to stay on near Him for almost a whole year in 1993. It gave us time to contemplate these declarations. I realized how ardently and desperately many of us were trying to understand and experience these basic truths that Swami conveys. He also explains to us that these declarations are meant to "put you on the direct flight to your destination."

The supreme dharma of a human being is to move to our destination, to return permanently to our source. But we have to be perfectly clear: What is our destination? What is our source? Swami gives us crystal clear directions:

*Destroy the identification of the self with the body. Get firm in the belief that all this is Paramatma and nothing else. There is nothing else to be done except bowing to His Will and surrendering to His Plan. This is the sum of your duty.*

*Your primary duty should be to become the masters of yourselves, to hold intimate and constant communion with the Divine that is in you as well as in the universe of which you are a part.*

When we pray to Swami for guidance, He invariably responds. I would like to share the experience of how He resolved my dilemma on these three fundamental declarations.

It all happened in August 1993. I was to interact with the devotees during the lectures that were part of the daily routine. I felt an inner compulsion to focus on these three declarations. But how? I did not know.

Two days before I was due to speak, I woke up, as usual, very early in the morning in the guest house in Brindavan. Sitting in bed for contemplation, I prayed to Baba: "Swami, do please guide me to explain your three declarations in some simple way, so simple that even a 'slow kid' like me would understand." Having thus prayed, I turned around in my bed to face Baba's house, Trayee, as if Swami's presence was confined to that little building! That is what the force of habit does to us. I sat quietly, I do not know for how long. Suddenly, like a flash, Swami put a thought in my mind - *ice cubes*. It was another riddle. What had ice cubes to do with divinity? I was completely confused. But then, over the years, I learned that when I am stuck and pray to Swami, "Please handle it, Baba, I just cannot," He shows the way.

On this occasion, the guidance led to a simple demonstration. It starts with me showing the audience a glass container full of ice cubes and water (see Figure 1). An imaginary conversation takes place between the water and the ice cubes.

> **Water**: "Ice cubes, I am always with you. I am all around you, I am on your left, on your right, in front of you, at your back, above you and below you."

After a little pause, I ask the audience if the statement made by the water is true or not. Invariably, the response is positive because people can see the truth of the statement with their own eyes. Then water speaks again:

> **Water**: "Ice cubes, you are in me and I am in you."

# THE GREAT DELUSION

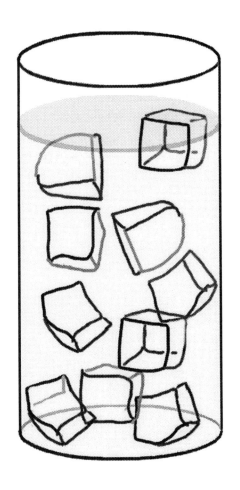

**Figure 1**

Once again, after a little pause, I ask the audience if the statement made by the water is true. There is an even more enthusiastic "yes." Everyone knows that ice cubes are frozen water. Finally, water speaks its last sentence:

**Water:** "Ice cubes, I am water. You are also water; we are one."

The audience readily accepts this also to be true. Then the ice cubes respond to the declarations made by the water. A few of them speak:

**First Ice Cube:** I am not water. I am an ice cube. I am the most perfect and the most beautiful form in the whole universe. All my sides are equal and each side is at a perfect right angle to the other. How could anyone even imagine that I am mere water?" Then with great pride and deliberation, he repeats," I am an ice cube."

**Second Ice Cube:** "Brother, what you say is absolutely true. But don't forget, I am very special. I am an Indian ice cube, very ancient, well-versed in Vedic wisdom."

**Third Ice Cube:** "Well, well, well. Don't forget, I am an American ice cube, from the number one nation in the world. I am more special than anyone here."

**Fourth Ice Cube,** squeezing his way up front and saying in a slow drawl: "I am sure you all have heard of the small check of only $9 million that I have donated for the hospital."

So an intense cacophony goes on among the ice cubes. Ignorant of the reality that all of them are water, they are so obsessed with their temporary identity that they have no time to even pause and ask the question, "Who am I?"

At this stage of the demonstration, the audience is ready and eager for the next part. This is in the form of an explanation.

Just as a glass container is full of water and ice cubes float in it, the entire universe is full of a formless power or force in which floats all that we can perceive - the galaxies, solar systems, suns, planets, and moons, including a little speck called planet Earth and all that exists on it. The power or force cannot be seen with the eyes, but numerous spiritual scientists, who have experienced its omnipresent, omnipotent, and omniscient presence, have labeled this power differently: God, I, Self, Brahman, Allah, Tao, Supreme Creator, Chu, Om, Over-Soul, Atma, Divinity, Field, Paramatma, and so on.

Perhaps the most functional label for this power, which is also Sai Baba's favorite label, is *Sat-chit-anand*. It means that this power or force that is filling the universe and beyond has three attributes: *sat*, the sub-stratum (the raw material), the substance (the product meaning the universe), the separate and the sum forms the indestructable permanence; *chit*, awareness, the activity (like seeing and hearing), the consciousness, feeling, the willing and doing; and *anand*, the harmony and melody, the enduring bliss. Just as water is wet, liquid, and transparent at the same time, this power called God is Sat-chit-anand at the same time. These attributes cannot be separated.

Just as the raw material for ice cubes is water, the raw material for all that we perceive in the universe is this power labeled God.

Just as ice cubes are a temporary form of water, all that we perceive is the temporary form of the formless power or force labeled God or Sat-chit-anand.

Spiritual scientists experienced this truth thousands of years ago, and now even physical science in its infancy is moving towards the same conclusion.

For example, Newtonian physics has been overtaken by subparticle physics. It is now well accepted that all matter is temporarily condensed energy[3] and that all galaxies and solar systems have a birth, a life span and death, reverting back to the permanent source (i.e. energy). David Bohm, an eminent quantum mechanics professor, says that the entire matter in the universe is equivalent to merely one cubic centimeter of energy of the wave length $10CM^{-32}$, or a wave length of .00000 00000 00000 00000 00000 00000 0000001 centimeter. He is merely reiterating what Sai Baba said as Krishna in the *Bhagavad Gita,* "All the universe is merely a particle of reality," or for that matter what He says now, "All the universe is in this hand."

When Jim Crutchfield, a professor of chaos systems at the University of California at Berkeley, says that "the gravitational pull of an electron randomly shifting position at the edge of the Milky Way can change the outcome of a billiard game on Earth," he is merely restating Sai Baba's words when He says that the entire universe is "My indivisible and interconnected body."

When we understand that we are divine, that in fact we are no different than God, then doing and living our dharma comes naturally to us. Then we understand the real meaning of Swami's advice:

> *One has to ask oneself whether the activity he chooses will benefit the country and the society. He can then be directed by the answer and derive maximum result from his knowledge, strength and skill.*

If the truth as to who we are is so simple, then why do we not comprehend such an easy reality? Why do we persist in behaving as if we were different and very special ice cubes?

---

[3]Energy or *shakti* is an aspect of the attribute "sat," meaning indestructible permanence. Energy can change form but cannot be destroyed.

The iron curtain that hides this simple truth from us is selfishness. It is often called individualism to lend it respectability!

Many years ago when I had the privilege of discussing with Swami selflessness as the foundation for effective leadership, He cautioned me, "Don't forget that selfishness is human and selflessness is divine." He went on to add, "There are some people coming here for the last fifty years, but there is absolutely no change in them." This left me in some doubt. Is selflessness really the key or was I chasing an illusion? Swami created a situation to clear this doubt.

It was early November 1991, hardly ten days before the Super Specialty Hospital was to be inaugurated. Around-the-clock feverish activity was in progress. Machines were being flown in from all parts of the world; floors were being given their final polish; doctors were testing their state-of-the-art equipment. This gigantic hospital had been built in just five months. That morning, Swami came out of the interview room and went straight to the university students. He was carrying a letter in his hand. He explained to them that the President of India, Mr. Venkatraman, had written that the construction of the hospital in just five months was a miracle. Had it been done by the Government of India, it would have taken five years! Having spoken to the boys, Swami was walking back to the interview room. When He passed me, I prayed to Him that the building of the hospital in five months would be an excellent case study on leadership for the management students. He paused, turned around, looked at me for a while and then raised His eyes to the far horizon. He said, "No, not any management" and recited a Sanskrit *sloka*:

*Na karmana, no parajaya, dhanenna*
*Thyagenaike amrutatwa manshu*

*Not by action, not by progeny, not by wealth but by sacrifice alone can immortality be achieved.*

My lingering doubt about the supreme importance of selflessness was removed. The key word in the above stanza is *thyaga*. Its meaning is a combination of sacrifice, selflessness and giving up of attachments.

If we have to break the iron curtain of selfishness that prevents us from understanding our reality, then the first step that we have to take is to analyze the full composition of selfishness (See Figure 2).

Desire, or call it want if you will, is the mother. Its children form the outer ring of the network. When we do not get what we want, we become angry and jealous; and if we do get what we want, then we get attached to what we get. Then we become greedy for more, and slowly our egotism inflates to fantastic dimensions. The result is that our decision to do anything depends entirely on one single consideration: "What am I going to get out of it?" This me-first syndrome becomes a habit, and it's very difficult to break out of it. The iron curtain of our mind, which Swami often describes as the "cataract of the mind," keeps on becoming stronger and thicker. Is there a way to break through it? Is there a way to reverse the cataract? There is. This is what *sadhana* (spiritual discipline) is all about. There is a very interesting episode related to this.

During our visit to the United States in 1991, I picked up a best seller on leadership entitled *The Seven Habits of Highly Effective People*. I was excited because on page 46 of the book, there is a quote which the author calls an ancient maxim. This quote forms the theme of the entire book. He does not mention where he found this maxim, but I was happy because it is an ancient piece of Indian wisdom which I had come across in a book entitled *Self Knowledge* by Swami Sivananda. I was happy that this ancient Indian finding was influencing American minds and, therefore, doing good for humanity. I carried the book to Puttaparthi in November 1991 as Swami's birthday was nearing. I wanted to show this discovery to Him. I always had the book with me when I went for darshan. A few

# NETWORK OF SELFISHNESS

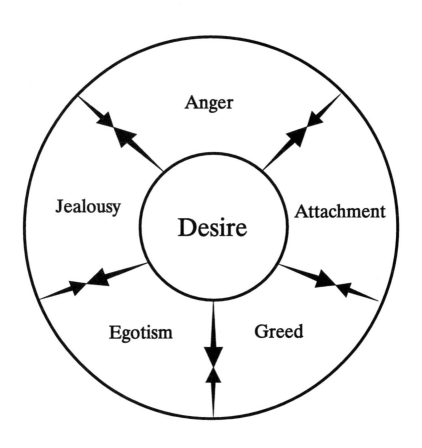

## Figure 2

days before the birthday, we had the good fortune of receiving an interview. During the private interview, I was waiting anxiously to open the page and, when I did so, Swami ignored it. I thought that was the end of wanting to share this discovery with Baba. But was it?

That year Swami had invited the new Prime Minister of India, P.V. Narasima Rao, for the convocation of the University. In His convocation discourse, Swami lambasted the Government for commercializing health care and education, the two primary duties of any democratic government. He ended His discourse with the ancient wisdom that I was so eager to show him:

*Take care of your thoughts. Then actions will take care of themselves. You sow an action and reap a tendency. You sow a tendency and reap a habit. You sow your character and reap your destiny. Therefore, destiny is in your own hands.*

Swami concluded His address by explaining that the key to control over destiny was our mind. As with a lock, if we turn the key toward the outer world, we lock out the vision of our reality. On the other hand, if we turn the key inward toward our reality, then the lock opens and who we are starts becoming clearer.

On finishing the discourse, Swami returned to His seat. I was sitting right behind Him as a member of the University Academic Council. Swami had given me a vision of the reality, for who had articulated this ancient wisdom? Who was Swami Sivananda who rendered this ancient wisdom into English during the mid-30s? Who was the American author who had written this best seller? Who was General Chibber who thought he had made a great discovery and wanted to show it to its very source? What was the book on which these words were printed? All were, like the ice cubes, temporary forms of the *one* formless reality, sat-chit-anand. I sat there in great bliss. To what lengths does Swami go to administer the therapy that a spiritual patient needs! All I could do was to say a silent "Thank you, Swami," and enjoy the thrill of His love. When Swami quotes verbatim pages and verses from books He has never physically seen, He is merely giving us a demonstration of the chit component (universal consciousness, omniscience) of our own reality.

Is there a simple formula to help us change our habits, to turn the key, the mind, in the right direction? A human "ice cube" who had experienced his own reality about 100 years ago articulated the formula. He was a guy named Swami Vivekananda. He said:

*I cannot ask everybody to be totally selfless; it is just not possible. But if you cannot think of humanity, at least think of your country. If you cannot think of your country, at least think of your community. If you cannot think of your community, think of your family. If you cannot think of your family, at least think of your wife. But for heaven's sake, do not think merely of yourself.*

Vivekananda advisedly left God out of the picture! He knew that anyone who rises to the ideal of thinking of humanity will automatically be grabbed by God by the collar and pulled up to experience His reality! That is why Swami has declared:

*Fill the brain with high thoughts, highest ideals; place them day and night before you, and out of that will come great work.*

As we raise our ideals in life, our desires get converted from a quest for petty impermanent pleasures to a quest for nobler ones. The number of our desires also starts decreasing. As our desires change from personal worldly wants to higher ideals,

# COMPOSITION OF SELFLESSNESS
# THE SOURCE OF HUMAN VALUES

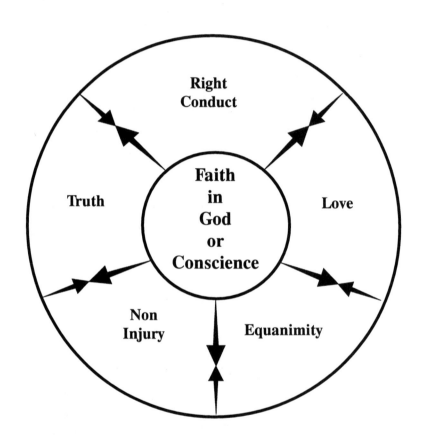

# Figure 3

we start breaking through the iron curtain that prevents us from seeing our reality. Our mental cataract becomes thinner and thinner. This spiritual growth, the ascent of man, is depicted in Figure 3. There is an interesting revelation in this diagram.

It is an important part of the Indian spiritual heritage that every ceremony, action or ritual that we undertake ends with one of the noblest prayers created by mankind. In Sanskrit this prayer is *Loka samastha suhki nau bhavantu*, meaning "May all beings in the world have peace and comfort." We parrot this prayer, but in our inner motives and in our conduct the prayer, in corrupted Sanskrit, would read *Loka samastha sukhi mum karantu*, meaning "May the entire world make me happy!"

Young people today have to live in a rough-and-tumble environment of cutthroat competition where the dictum is, "If he is smart, why isn't he rich?" Any talk of values is termed childish, or at best out-of-date Eastern mumbo-jumbo. Making a quick buck is the measure of success. The youngsters naturally ask questions, "What is there for me in this puzzle called dharma? I am not interested in the hereafter or the beyond. Do I get something here and now?"

The answer is yes. There is an immediate reward in reprogramming our minds and changing our habits and, consequently, our character. This reward is what is enshrined in the Declaration of Independence of the most powerful democracy in the world, the United States of America. This document contains the lofty ideal that every man has a right to "life, liberty, and the pursuit of happiness." However, pursuit of happiness has become the goal in the modern world. This goal is sought by satisfying our cravings and fulfilling our wants. The result is quite the opposite: We are rewarded with stress, envy, inner turmoil, and addiction to sleeping pills. This is so because want and craving is the cause of all suffering and wrongdoing.

Enduring happiness, as opposed to cycles of instant pleasure and intense pain, is guaranteed on the path of spiritual growth.

It is achieved by mounting a direct attack on the mother of selfishness - desire. This wisdom experienced by all civilizations of the world that have endured has been summed up in a simple mathematical equation. This equation was evolved by a young professor who, toward the end of the 19th century, was being sent to Cambridge University in England for research in higher mathematics. However, instead of going to Cambridge, he ended up at Rishikesh on the banks of the holy river Ganges as a renunciate and became Swami Ramtirath. He created this equation:

$$\text{Happiness} = \frac{\text{Number of desires fulfilled}}{\text{Number of desires entertained}}$$

Many people who have read the *Upanishads* jump to the conclusion that if we make the number of desires entertained as zero, then we achieve liberation and eternal bliss. That indeed is the declaration in the *Taittriyopanishad II*, 8th stanza.[4] It is perhaps this stanza which motivated the gifted mathematician to invent the equation for people like us who want peace and happiness here and now.

All that the equation conveys is that if we can control and reduce the number of worldly desires that we entertain, then our happiness quotient goes up. For example, if I have the health, ability, education, and resources to fulfill four desires, then my happiness quotient will vary as shown below:

---

[4]This stanza means "If all the pleasures of the world are equal to one unit, then the happiness and bliss which is within each human being can be experienced by renouncing desires equal to 10 units[22]." A human being enjoys one unit of worldly pleasures when "he is young, well-educated, well-disciplined, mentally resolute, physically strong and comes to possess the whole world's riches and its joys."

|  |  |  | **Happiness Quotient** |
|---|---|---|---|
| If I entertain 16 desires then | $H = \dfrac{4}{16}$ | $=$ | .25 |
| If I entertain 8 desires then | $H = \dfrac{4}{8}$ | $=$ | .5 |
| If I entertain 4 desires then | $H = \dfrac{4}{4}$ |  | 1 |
| If I entertain 2 desires then | $H = \dfrac{4}{2}$ |  | 2 |

Knowing that many of us get tied up in knots at the simplest arithmetic problem, Swami guides us toward the same end by wanting us to "place a ceiling on desires." What does it all mean? The message for our day-to-day life is loud and clear. We must discriminate between needs and wants and then control our wants. For example, stainless steel cutlery is a need to eat food in the West, but to have silver or gold implements is a want and in no way changes the taste of the food. To succeed in reducing our wants, we have to resist the highly skilled psychological onslaught of visual advertising, particularly on television. And we have to resist the cancer of keeping up with the Joneses. As we succeed in this endeavor and start discovering the composition of selflessness, our conduct changes to reflect that composition. This composition is shown in Figure 4. These are the values which Swami has incarnated to restore to mankind.

As we grow from selfishness to selflessness, our dharmic dilemmas become less and less. Selfless man is neither greedy

# THE ASCENT OF MAN

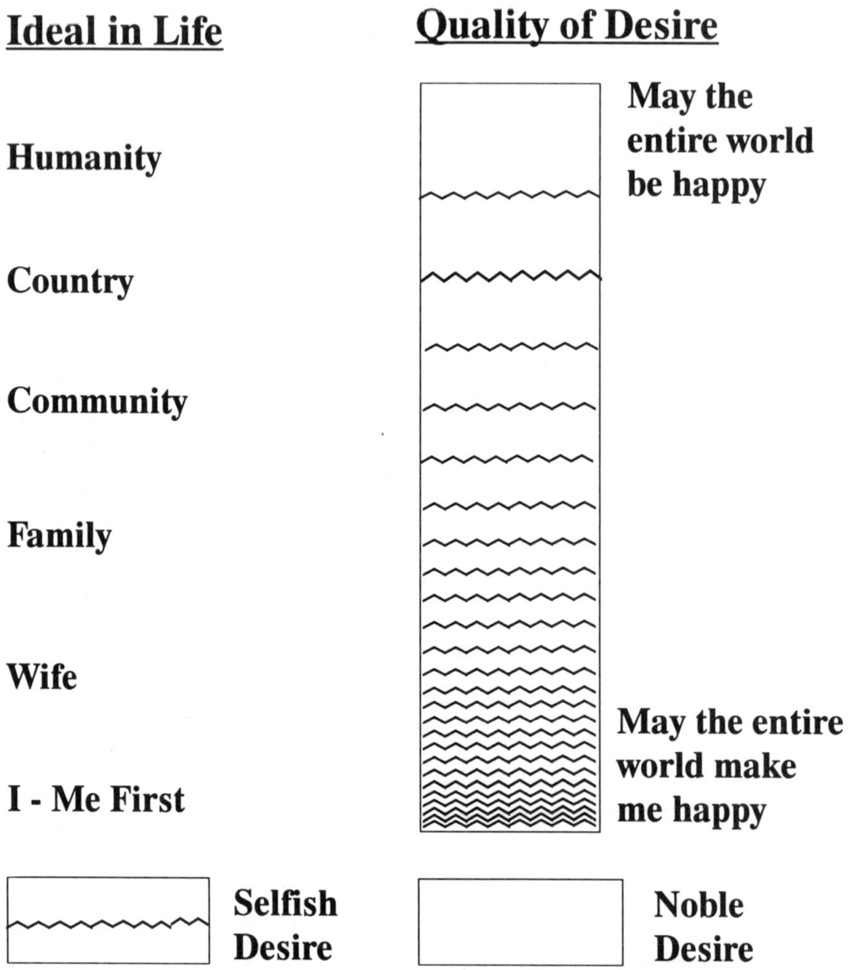

**Ideal in Life**　　　　**Quality of Desire**

Humanity

May the
entire world
be happy

Country

Community

Family

Wife

I - Me First

May the entire
world make
me happy

Selfish
Desire

Noble
Desire

## Figure 4

nor looking for short cuts to success; hence his integrity never wavers. He seeks no unfair advantage over others; honesty comes naturally to him. He is not a self-seeker; therefore, his loyalty is steady and strong. When a man has these virtues, then his thoughts, words, and deeds become well integrated. He says what he thinks and does what he says. There is no "double-speak" or "double standard" in his nature. That establishes his credibility and he is trusted. In short, he becomes the living model of the five values taught by Baba: truth, right action, love, peace, and nonviolence.

As mentioned earlier, my wife and I have often verbally complained to Swami about our coming to Him so late. I once grumbled, "Swami, how can I, at this late stage, understand and then experience that 'I am I.' It is too late in life." He looked amused and merely said, "No, no, there is time. You try." Thus the ball is squarely in my court. Indeed, that is the case with everyone whom Swami has willed to come into His presence. The only free will we have is to transform ourselves to understand and then experience our reality. When we take one step toward Him (our reality), Swami responds with ten steps toward us. We then derive great joy in living our real dharma, which in Sai Baba's words is to:

*See God in everyone you meet; see God in everything you handle. Live together, revere each other; let not the seeds of envy and hate grow and choke the clear stream of love.*

More than 5,000 years ago, Sai Baba was around on this planet as Krishna. He had physically participated in the famous battle of Mahabharatha as the strategic advisor to the Pandavas. After their victory, he took the Pandavas to the legendary hero, Bhishma, who lay dying on the battlefield. He asked Bhishma to advise the Pandavas on how to rule well, how to be good leaders. (If anyone now concludes that it was He Himself as Krishna who advised Himself as the Pandavas and then took them to Himself as Bhishma, whom He spoke through, then he is dead right. It was He who as the puppeteer wrote this story and then moved the hand of this puppet to add this final paragraph!) Bhishma then gave the most seminal advice to the Pandavas. The last part of this advice is the beacon light for meeting all dharmic challenges:

*Man is born alone and he dies alone. He has not a single companion on his march through this incident called life. The spouse, the father, the mother, sons, kinsmen, friends, all turn away from your body and go about their work. Only dharma follows the body. That is the only enduring friend of man, and the only thing he should seek.*

# A MOTHER'S STORY
### Sandra Levy

*What then is the meaning of spirituality? It is not the reading of scriptures or the performance of rituals. It is to live up to the truth one has learnt.*

I realize now that nothing in my life has been such a challenge in terms of *dharma* (which in my limited understanding means both right conduct and being true to one's own innate nature) as parenting.

Certainly, it has been an experience for which I was totally unprepared in many ways and for which I stubbornly resisted any advice.

Although this was partly ego - the need to prove myself as a modern mother - and partly social conditioning, there was also a spiritual motive underlying it. At least, the path I found myself on was very much like a spiritual path. I had to discard all my expectations, hopes, and wishes, accept reality, set my own ego aside, and bravely go into the unknown, learning the disciplines and skills required as I went along.

To understand why I made such heavy weather of it all, you should know that before this I was not a very down-to-earth person. I loved reading and drawing, was basically a dreamer, and had, since my postwar London childhood, many unanswered questions about the meaning of life. By the time I was in my 20s, I was lucky enough to find a husband who was on the same spiritual quest (but who was, mercifully, much more practical and sensible than I was) and who introduced me to the philosophy classes he was attending. I was delighted with these classes, which embraced the hidden and ageless wisdom of all religions and the arts. We learned how to meditate, heard about self-realization and what an *avatar* was, although I never in my wildest dreams thought I would ever meet one.

So when it came to having my first child, I was full of wonderful idealistic ideas about children and motherhood, best expressed by that beautiful poem in *The Prophet* by Khalil Gibran, which inspired so many of my generation:

*Your children are not your children.*
*They are the children of life's longing for itself.*
*And they come through you but not from you.*
*And though they are with you yet they belong not to you.*
*You may give them your love but not your thoughts...*
*You may house their bodies but not their souls,*
*For their souls dwell in the house of tomorrow,*
*Which you cannot visit, even in your dreams.*

The actual experience of being a mother and coping with my first child thrust me into everyday life and surprised me with turbulent feelings I thought I'd dealt with in childhood. Here is a poem I wrote soon after Andrew was born:

*Another creature was born when my son arrived.*
*He was a stranger to me; she was even stranger.*
*Did things I never did, heard sounds no one else did*
*Awoke, psychic, before the first cry; discovered*
*The inner horror as well as the out-reaching tenderness.*
*Spat shrieks of flash-hate, then buried the resulting guilt.*
*My son grows healthier each day;*
*How will this creature grow?*

I still believed in the words of *The Prophet*, but now I knew what the resistance was. For the next several years, my task became to blend my spiritual ideals with the daily realities, heavy responsibilities, and passionate personal attachments of being a parent.

I tried very hard to be a fair and reasonable mother, as well as a loving one: to have no favorites, respect my children's privacy, and encourage them without pushing them. And sometimes I failed and yelled at and nagged them. As they got older, they would give me their own unerring observations about my efforts: "Mum, we know you're a liberated parent, but you're still an old-fashioned mum underneath it all!"

When I first heard about Baba, years later, I was thrilled to know He existed, and started eagerly to read everything about him. Everyone has something they especially treasure about Baba, and the unique thing for me was that He expressed in His teachings, and, as I discovered later, in His every action, both intense love and detachment. He said glorious universal things, such as "There is only one religion, the religion of Love," and poignant, compassionate, personal things, such as "Bring me the depths of your mind, no matter how cruelly ravaged by doubt and disappointment. I know what to do with them; I am your Mother." He understood. He was not a remote, moralizing guru. He actually acknowledged and contained both of those opposite human qualities I'd been grappling with for so long.

The first group interview I attended, in 1984, held a powerful dharmic lesson for all of us. One of our group members had actually died during the pilgrimage, a lovely young woman who had leukemia and who had come with her mother and doctor hoping for a healing. How we had all prayed for Lorraine! We were hoping for a miracle, and we felt sure that such a young woman, with a young baby and husband waiting for her return, deserved to be healed. But it was not the miracle we had prayed for. Lorraine was healed spiritually but not physically. Baba was so kind to her mother in that interview, kind but firm. Lorraine was with Him now, He said, but her ashes could be buried in the holy Chitravatri river, and He gave the mother a beautiful nine-stone ring to protect and console her. And so I learned that when you pray, you don't try to impose your will on God: you pray for the best and highest outcome and surrender all your hopes and fears to the One who sees the whole picture. That intense, human love is very close to willfulness sometimes.

During another interview, in 1989, Baba gave us another lesson on motherhood. A young widow with two teenage sons to raise asked for His blessing. Baba picked up a photo of one of them and said, "Yes, naughty boy. I will help, but you must do your duty. Sometimes you love too much. You must love, but not too much love. Body temperature normal at 98 degrees - at 99 degrees, fever. Eyes see with light, but too much light damages the retina. Life is a limited company." More insights, guidance about controlling our mother love.

When we love, we should not abdicate our discrimination, our intelligence, our common sense. And the balance between right action and harm is so fine sometimes that it takes constant integrated awareness[1] to maintain.

Of course, you don't have to be a biological mother to 'mother' people - to nurture and care for them, to encourage them and comfort them when things go wrong, while respecting their individuality. Most people do this in various ways in their daily lives, and this is what my husband and I have tried to do over the past eight years in the course of taking groups to India for Baba's *darshan*. Each trip has presented its own unique challenges and lessons, and one of the most challenging was the time we were due to take a group to Prasanthi Nilayam on what turned out to be the second day of the Gulf War.

As the political situation built up the week before we went away, I found myself justifying our going to my mother and others: "Yes, of course we're still going. We're in touch with our travel agent all the time, and we know all the airlines are still operating. We're not traveling on an American, Israeli, or

---

[1]The higher faculty of immediate comprehensive cognition. Truth reveals itself to us in a flash of immediate apprehension, without the intermediary of the mind soiling that truth with its conceptualization and web-spinning imagination.

Gulf airline; that would be different." One part of me felt sure that if Baba had called us to Him at that time, then that was the best thing for us to do. I knew I had to have faith in Baba, whatever happened. But my faith was a more realistic faith by then: it was faith that whatever happened would be for the best according to everyone's karma and that Baba would give us all the strength to go through it. I must say another part of me was secretly hoping some of the group would cancel and my husband would decide to postpone the trip. To my amazement, admiration, and chagrin, not one of the 50 group members canceled.

A few days before we left, my mother sent me a most persuasive letter, telling me to think of her and my sister and my children and not go to India when war was about to break out. She was convinced the war would consume the whole East; I couldn't blame her especially as she'd had the awful experience of going through World War II as a young woman. I told her that our plane was going to fly over Russia and Turkey to avoid the war zone. But when the media reported that Iraqis were beginning to fire missiles at Saudi Arabia and Israel, I was far from confident myself.

This was a challenge people all over the world were facing. Life does not stop during a political crisis; you carry on with your work as far as you are able and fulfill your promises to others.

The day before we left, the television news showed a film of tanks at Heathrow Airport, just miles from my home. I really had to face my worse fears, which centered around the possibility of our plane being hijacked. I kept imagining we would be picked out of the passenger list by our obviously Jewish name and tortured, killed, or held hostage. Then I remembered a saying of Swami's: "Follow the master (the conscience), face the devil, fight to the end, finish the game."

"Facing the devil" for me in this situation meant thinking through the fears, being prepared to accept that they might happen, and then praying for strength to get through the situation in the most dignified manner.

Once I did that, I didn't feel so stuck. I did wake up with an awful lurch in my stomach on the morning of the flight and in the taxi to Heathrow, when the news came straight through on the radio that more scuds had been fired, that the Iraqis obviously still had plenty of ammunition after the initial counterattack. I quickly turned to my fellow traveller in the taxi and started to talk about Swami, everything I knew and had experienced about him. It took our minds off our fear and stopped us from hearing any more scary news.

As it happened, there were no tanks at Heathrow (it must have been a propaganda exercise) and our flight to Bombay that day was one of the smoothest ever.

When we asked Swami in the interview room, "What about the Gulf War, Swami?," Baba tapped his chest and said, "Inner war, that's what you should be concerned about."

Another important trip was at the time of the Ayodhya shrine riots in 1992. We had all three of our grown sons with us on this trip. It was the first time they had ever been to India and they wanted to travel around for a few weeks, then join us at Prasanthi Nilayam the week before Christmas. So we planned that they should stay in Bombay while we took the rest of the group of 80 on to Bangalore.

We heard about the destruction of the Ayodhya shrine on the plane to Bangalore. By the time we were installed in a hotel, we began to hear about the widespread riots that had begun in several places, including Bombay. Members of our group kept saying, "Don't worry, I'm sure Baba will look after your boys." Although I was glad of our friends' support, privately I knew, both from the reality of the situation and from experience of Baba, that it was wrong to assume any such thing. And although I hoped and prayed for Baba to watch over the boys, I knew it was quite possible one or all of them could be injured or even killed. Why should my children be any different? Perhaps it was a big test for me.

While keeping a calm and cheerful front to others, my fantasies about what might happen to the boys were over the top. To make things worse, we were in a big modern hotel which had satellite television, so we could watch BBC World News every hour, and we could see for ourselves riot police, empty streets, fires in Calcutta, Delhi, and other cities and towns all over India.

Then suddenly I said to myself, "What am I doing, feeding these dark thoughts? Everyone knows the power of thought!" I realized I had a choice of getting sucked completely into my fears and communicating them to my boys, or I could consciously change those thoughts to positive ones. I remembered someone asking Baba in an interview once, "Baba, what should I do about bad thoughts?" Baba had answered, "What do you do when there is a bad smell? You replace it with a good smell. So with bad thoughts."

After that, every time I found myself thinking of the boys, I would visualize them happy and safe, with a cloud of peach-colored light around them.

As it happened, the boys did get safely to Prasanthi Nilayam a week before Christmas, having had many difficult and dangerous experiences, and we all had a wonderful reunion. They had managed to get to Goa where there were no riots and had spent most of the time there.

Some of the most difficult decisions we have to make are those where there is a conflict of responsibilities. In October 1993, we had just arrived with a group of 100 people in Prasanthi Nilayam when we heard that the mother of Aimé, my husband, was dangerously ill in the hospital. She had been ill before we'd left London, but was still up and about and able to care for herself. This was a rapid deterioration and came as a big shock to us. I remember thinking, I wonder if we'll have to go home in the middle of the trip. But Aimé had already decided: "We'll go home tomorrow morning. Let's start packing now." We packed our bags and cleared the flat, briefed our eight capable group sub-leaders, and booked a taxi to leave after darshan.

But before we set off that morning, I decided I would feel better if I had Baba's blessing to return. I'd never asked for special permission to have a first line position at darshan before, but I felt this was an unusual emergency. I asked the head volunteer and she agreed. I sat there, in my best temple sari, with a letter to hand to Swami asking his blessing to go back - and He made a complete detour around me. I remember thinking ruefully, "Well, we have already made our arrangements to go; it isn't as if we are unsure about what we should do." As it happened, our dear Mémé passed on only 18 hours after we arrived at her bedside. Although in a coma by then, she waited for us, for her sister from the United States, and for our son, who came back unexpectedly from a holiday in France. One night after the funeral, when I was unable to sleep because of stress and jet lag and grief, I sat down in my meditation room and drew just one card from the box of Swami's sayings. This was the message on the card:

*I sometimes act as if I keep you at a distance; this is done only to reform you more quickly. When a stretch of road is being repaired, I go by a detour, and I do not use that bit of road for some time. The purpose is to let the repair works proceed more quickly so that I may use that road again.*

I still carry that card in my purse. An avatar does not waste time patting you on the back when He knows you've already made a dharmic decision.

When one of my sons was ill just before we were due to go on a trip, I did have an agonizing time worrying about him and trying to get him into the hospital. Of course, this was not a dependent child but a young man of 26 who was already living on the other side of London near his fiancée. Nevertheless, I was consumed with anxiety, and four days before we were due to go to India I prayed desperately, imploring Baba, "Baba, please! Do something!"

The very same night, the illness came to a crisis and my son was admitted to the hospital. What's more, because his local hospital had no free bed that evening, he was taken at no cost to a private hospital, which had many more facilities and was incidentally much nearer to my home. Never was I so convinced that Baba had answered a prayer in the most immediate and compassionate way. I knew my son was in good hands and that I would be much more useful helping Aimé with the pilgrimage, and I prepared to go on the trip. But even with a dramatic sign like that, I was still plagued with doubt and guilt, especially when one of my son's friends declared, "I think Aimé should go, but Sandra should stay behind." Much later, I realized that it wasn't even guilt that plagued me so much as fear of what others might think of me - pretty low criteria.

Synchronicity is one of Swami's most powerful teaching aids. In the same month that I finished writing this piece on parenting, my three sons moved into their own place together, which has given us all more space, physical and psychological. The house that finally came up to all their exacting requirements (near the trains and shops, etc.) happened to have the street address of 108, and they moved in a few days after I returned from a trip to Brindavan, the highlight of which was witnessing a wonderful dance based on the 108 Names[2] performed in front of Swami by *Bal Vikas*

---

[2] Of all the sacred numbers, 108 is the one most immediately associated with Baba, because of the ancient Hindu tradition of reciting the 108 names of God, and because with Baba's advent, a special "garland" of 108 names or attributes was composed specifically for him.

children from the United Kingdom. The best scene for me was a most moving enactment of Swami telling his mother Easwaramma that He was no longer her son, but belonged to His devotees; His mission had begun.

In spite of all the jokes I had made about pushing the overgrown offspring out of the nest, tears filled my eyes as I watched Easwaramma pleading with her son to stay, and young Swami, so calm, so loving, firmly insisting on going.

So begins a new phase in my efforts to love and let go, to love and respect the divine in my children and in everyone I meet, and yet stand aside as each pursues their own mission in life. I'll be praying for some of that constant integrated awareness and for Swami to help me up again when I fall.

# WATCH
## Judy Warner

Swami tells us to W-A-T-C-H our Words, Actions, Thoughts, Character, and Heart. This is not an entirely new concept for me. I grew up with these high ideals. My father, a New York State Supreme Court Judge, made obeying the law, telling the truth, and being honest in every way a very real part of my life. I remember that my father wouldn't even take a pack of cigarettes from a friend for fear they would want a favor from him. As a judge's daughter, I was expected to carry on this legacy.

Since coming to Sathya Sai Baba, I have been shocked at myself for displaying, from time to time, questionable behavior and, even more, for my desires to be dishonest in quite a few situations. The amazing thing is that it is in the ashram where these temptations are the strongest. Not at home, but right there in the Abode of Peace! Why there, you may ask? I think it is because the need to be physically close to Swami is so strong that I rationalize my poor behavior. I simply forget when I see Him walking among us that He is omnipresent.

On one of my first visits to Baba, a good friend of mine was assigned to a tiny room with six other women. When their bedding was laid out on the floor, there wasn't even a space to walk. She was very upset and told me of her suffering. About a week later, all of her roommates were leaving. She was very happy because they offered to leave the room key with her without informing the office.

"Keep it," I said. "Spend a few days on your own. The office won't know." Within an hour, I realized what I had said. I searched the ashram until I found her and told her, "What I said to you was not dharmic (right action). I'm sorry. And it wasn't any of my business either. I just got caught up in your suffering because we're friends." Of course she understood. I never asked her after that what she chose to do as it had nothing to do with me.

The second time I remember being dishonest was also on one of my early trips. For the first few years, if my husband and I couldn't get a room in the ashram to ourselves, we lived in the village where the accommodations are more comfortable, but the vibration is not sacred. I was never comfortable with this, but did it anyway. When we were leaving that time, I went to the ashram accommodations office to get vibhuti. The man asked me, "What room were you living in?"

"R2 D6," said I, using the number of the ashram room my friend was staying in.

I was totally devastated by my lying. It just flew out of my mouth. Furthermore, I didn't even need vibhuti since Swami had given us an interview that year and had given us many small vibhuti packets. I was upset with myself for a long time. Finally, I realized what this lie was telling me: I had felt guilty about living in the village, and from then on, I needed to live inside the ashram, no matter what the accommodations.

Swami tells us we must not be animals but first must rise to at least the human level, and then finally to the divine. When I watch people, even those I know, jump lines in the ashram to get in front of others, I am amazed. Seeing people do this makes it harder for me to abide by the rules. I want to rationalize that it is okay to do this in these circumstances and this culture. But I remind myself that who I am today is what I will become tomorrow. I have thought many times of jumping lines, especially during festivals when it is very crowded. I keep hearing in my mind, "Do unto others as you want them to do unto you," so I try not to fall prey to this "animal tendency."

The procedure before darshan is for men and women, each in their own section, to line up in rows. Then the first person in each line draws a numbered chit out of a bag, which determines the order that the lines go into the temple grounds. During darshan, when Baba comes out to walk through the crowd, take letters, give blessings, and talk with people, often people stand up, blocking those behind them so they cannot see Him. Or they come from the back, climbing over rows of people, to give Swami a letter. I, too, have wanted to do this. I have watched myself for years, witnessing my own desire to think of myself first.

One morning during the Christmas season, as large numbers of us were lining up, a woman I know (who lives in the ashram now) was too late to get in the regular lines. However, she wouldn't get in the late line, where there were already about 50 people and which always goes in last. Instead, smiling sweetly and talking in an ingratiating manner, she stood near the *seva dals* (service volunteers), who wouldn't let her in to the other lines. It was as if she felt she were more important than the other 50 waiting women and therefore didn't have to be subjected to the same rules. Just as the numbers were being picked from the bag, a seva dal noticed a woman with a large pocketbook and told her she couldn't go into darshan with it, and to please leave her place in line. Then she signaled to my friend and told her to sit in this woman's place. My friend was very happy and had no apparent guilt feelings for going ahead of 50 people. I just watched.

"This is Swami's play," I thought. "But where is truth, where is dharma?"

All of a sudden I saw she was getting up. Her number had been picked; she would be in the first row! I heard her say, "Thank you, Baba." Of course, she was right. It is all His doing. But what about the dharma on this worldly level?

When I see behavior like this rewarded, I find it very confusing. So confusing, in fact, that I have given up trying to understand. I am learning slowly, very slowly, to accept whatever happens as His play. Baba taught me a lesson that really helped me with this.

I was in darshan in Madras, seated toward the front but way on the side, not near the aisle where Swami walks. I was sitting next to an Indian woman and her handicapped son. I offered her some vibhuti, which she took with enthusiasm, and with abandon she smeared it all over her son's twisted legs and torso. We smiled happily at each other, feeling our shared love of Sai.

A hush fell over the auditorium. Swami was walking in from the back. Suddenly, this woman took a letter from under her sari, gestured for her son to stay, and proceeded with great determination to climb over about 25 people to get to the center aisle. I watched, riveted to her need to get Swami's help for her son. She arrived at the center aisle just in time to give Baba her note. I was deeply moved. For the first time, I **knew** that I could not judge from the outside whether someone was acting correctly or not. I had to stop judging and, again, mind my own business - leaving everyone to their own dharmic choices and challenges. I realized that there is another legacy I have inherited - the Judge! This one has to be gotten rid of! If you think I've been hard on others, imagine how strictly I must judge myself.

The morning darshan of New Year's Day, I was in one of the last lines to be seated. I was stuck in the corner farthest from where Swami walks. I found a vacant chair in that corner and thought to myself, "I might as well sit here. Maybe the person won't come and I'll be able to see something. If she comes, wherever I end up sitting couldn't be worse than where I'd be now." I sat comfortably for about 20 minutes, noticing that the aisles were completely filled up and there was hardly a space on the ground. At 7 a.m. a ripple ran through the crowd: Baba was coming. At exactly the same time, from the other direction, an old woman, bent in two, was slowly moving in my direction. I wasn't sure if this was her chair or not, but knew I would give her my seat. I immediately got up for her.

Angry voices shouted, "Sit down!" "Sit down!" "Down!" "What does she think she's doing?" "Where are you going?" as I tried desperately to find a place to sit - anywhere - to get out of the way. No one would move an inch, but they continued shouting. Finally I spotted a ditch near a tree and headed in that direction. A woman had her leg stretched out with her foot resting in the ditch and, when I indicated that I was going to stoop down while leaning against the tree, she complained bitterly. With great reluctance and a dirty look, she removed her foot.

I remained in that painfully cramped position, unable to see Baba, until I was sure He was out of sight to the women's side. Barely able to struggle out of my contorted posture, I began to move again to try and find a seat on the ground. Again voices rose up, "Sit down!" "What are you doing?" "She's jockeying for a better position!" I couldn't believe the fury against me. Everyone actually believed I was looking for a better place when I was looking for **any** place. Finally an Indian woman picked up her child and placed her on her lap, giving me a tiny space to squeeze into. I was completely demolished, ready to burst into tears. I had ruined everyone's darshan, and everyone had misjudged me.

Controlling my tears, I realized, "This has got to be some lesson from Swami. I've never seen so many angry, selfish people all at once. This must have happened for a reason." By the end of the day, I had two incredible insights.

Just before leaving for India, I had said to my boss at the hospice where I am bereavement coordinator, "All the people I work with are always worried about what their neighbors think about them. Not me." I bragged, "If I feel I am doing the right thing, I do it. I never worry what someone will think of me."

I found out with this darshan experience just how deeply I **do care** what my Sai sisters think. I was hurt and distraught that they saw me as selfish and self-serving. It is clear to me now that I care what everyone thinks about me, not only my neighbors, but people I don't even know. Painful as this lesson was, it was an important one.

Although I have always listened to and been supportive of the people I work with, I never really understood this concern.

Now I do. I hope now when this issue is brought up, I am able to have real compassion for those I am serving.

I also realized again that you cannot judge from the outside what motivates a person. No one saw me get up and give my seat to the old woman, so they all assumed that I was selfish in trying to improve my position. Clearly, this was not the case.

I have also begun to understand that when I am judging others or myself, I am often making comparisons. I see that comparing myself to others is a form of jealousy. If I am content with who I am, where I am placed, would I ignore my neighbor's feelings in order to get what I want? I don't think so. As long as I have any jealousy, I cannot be totally dharmic. As a matter of fact, as long as I have any of the impurities[1] in me, I cannot act in a completely dharmic manner. For instance, when I told my friend to keep the key, I was feeling anger for her suffering. When I lied to get more vibhuti, I was feeling greed.

Of course, it is clear there is always something to be learned from these experiences, and it is clear we cannot judge what is really happening. I can only judge my own actions and be responsible for myself. It is impossible to judge the actions of others because there is no way to know what is motivating them. I have discovered that every situation where I do not act in a dharmic manner, it is because I have been motivated by self-interest.

The times when I do something spontaneously, forgetting myself, it can be truly a perfect action even though it may appear wrong to those watching. These are the actions that flow from Him, not from my own needs, desires or will.

One morning at darshan, I saw a beautiful example of this. An Australian group had been called by Baba for an interview and were sitting on the veranda. Baba came up, looked them

---

[1]Jealousy, pride, anger, hatred, lust, greed, attachment.

over, and went into His room. This was the moment that He would have sent any of them off the veranda if they were not to be there. All of a sudden, two women got up and left the veranda because they realized, I learned later, that this was not *their* Australian group. Frankly, I don't think I could have left once Swami had approved me. Too much greed! Yet it was obvious to me they did the dharmic thing. When I look at this action, I cannot see pride, jealousy, anger, hatred, lust, greed, or attachment of any kind - only right action that apparently flowed from Him.

At home in Virginia, the work I do in hospice helps to keep me ever watchful. As I see people die, it brings to mind the constant question, "Am I living my life in the right way for me?" This means, "Am I following Swami's teachings? Am I doing the work that is my duty? Am I doing it in the right spirit - dedicating everything to Swami with no eye on the fruits? Is the path of active service still my path, or should I now be leading a quieter life?" And, of course, the age-old question, "Who am I?" Working in hospice brings these larger questions out front for me to constantly examine.

Recently I had a dream in which a man was telling Swami how much He loved Him and how much He wanted to serve Him. After a long speech to Swami, he finally asked, "What kind of service should I be doing?" Swami smiled and, indicating to the man not to worry, said, "It is all illusion."

I have been thinking a lot about this. I believe Baba was saying two things to me: It doesn't matter what you do but how you do it. And, of even greater importance, we must get beyond these kinds of concerns and remember that we are God. The acts we perform are just the acting out of our roles in the play of life.

Only continual mindful awareness keeps me on the right track. It is the day-to-day challenges that are the hardest for me, for I find it hard to be mindful all the time. Quite often, I find myself falling back into old habits.

For instance, remaining patient has been one of my biggest challenges. This is so important because without patience it is impossible to act in an appropriate manner. Swami tells us, "Patience is all the strength a man needs." When I am working at the computer, I can get very impatient and annoyed when a program I'm very familiar with all of a sudden won't work correctly. I can feel the frustration rising in my stomach. I don't always overcome this frustration immediately; I can sit there really angry. Then, somehow, exhausted from this, I breathe and remember Swami. Then I'm able to pull back and remember that the fruit of the work is his, not mine; and, for the moment, I am free.

*Above all, do every act as an offering to the Lord, without being elated by success or dejected by defeat; this gives the poise and equanimity needed for sailing through the waters of the ocean of life.*

Judging others, measuring what they are doing or saying as right or wrong, is still a problem for me. Swami tell us, "All are good. If you see bad in them, it is because there is bad in you..." This judging of others happens particularly with those I am closest to and therefore most attached to. An example is that when my husband sometimes wants to watch a violent movie on TV, I find my mind running a mile a minute. "How can he watch all that violence? Baba says we must be careful what we put into our minds, and this is rubbish. How can he not listen to Swami about this? What kind of devotee is he really?" On and on these thoughts go. This serves no purpose other than to close out the love I feel for him. And who am I to judge him anyway? Maybe he is detached enough that he doesn't get affected by violence as I do. He has his own path that is different from mine. After all, doesn't Swami know what he's doing?! I have come to see that what I need at these moments is, first, to have forgiveness and compassion for myself for making this judgment. Then automatically I find that my love, compassion, and forgiveness return. What I do now, the minute I see my mind go into a critical mode, is make myself move to my heart, the place where there can be no judgment, only love and compassion. This works! But it takes a watchful eye and a certain amount of detachment.

Another trap I fall into all too often is thinking, "I'm the doer." Krishna proclaimed to Arjuna in the *Bhagavad Gita*, "Arjuna, you are only instrumental in the propagation of my message. You are just an instrument in my hands." This sense that I am the doer happens in many areas. For instance in my editing work, I can get attached to doing something my way. For example, I want a story to be expanded as I want and in the way I want, and other portions to be deleted that I don't think are relevant. My need to be in control becomes paramount, so much so that sometimes I become overbearing. The more out of control I feel, the more control I want. Now that I understand this pattern, almost the moment I get bossy, I can stop. I think to myself, "I must be feeling out of control. That's why I'm acting like this." Later, I realize, "Who is in control anyhow? Swami. Not me." I still fall into the trap, but as time goes on, I am getting out faster.

I have learned over the years that in order to have spiritual clarity, I must have a good deal of my emotional agenda worked out. This is a never-ending process, but with the help of the spiritual viewpoint, the emotions can be seen and experienced in a different light. We can see everything as "grist for the mill," rather than only as pain and suffering.

A few months ago, I realized that I couldn't really listen to my clients at the hospice. I was feeling sleepy during the appointments. Their pain was reflecting my own, and therefore sticking to me. This had never happened before, so I knew I had to deal with whatever was going on inside of me. I'm not one to let things go on for long; I'd rather meet the situation head on and go through the pain in order to come out feeling alive and clear again. After a lot of deep work, I felt centered and able to listen to my clients again without having their pain affect me. I have always felt that my ability to be able to do this hospice work is all Swami's grace. My small self could never listen to all the pain, suffering, grief, and rage that I hear. Swami makes me stay clear and centered and focused on His presence in order to do His work.

It has become clearer and clearer to me that being impatient, judgmental or feeling that I am the doer, or having any form of selfishness, makes it impossible to be a dharmic person. That is why it is so important to be ever aware and mindful.

How wonderful that Swami makes us see every impurity of ours. In telling us to WATCH our words, actions, thoughts, character, and heart, He makes us be meticulous witnesses to ourselves. Then He requires that we note our faults, let them go, don't repeat them, and ultimately forgive and love ourselves despite our imperfections. Then we can also love others. Hopefully, we can eventually experience that we are God, and knowing this will make us see, as Swami said in my dream, "It is all illusion." This is a huge task. But what a wonderful gift to be given - to undergo all these challenges at the feet of our beloved Sai.

# SWAMI'S WAKE-UP CALL:
## Integrity and Spirit at Work
Jack Hawley

A few years ago, Swami directed me to write a book on human values and spirit in management, tentatively entitled *Dharmic Management.* At first I thought it would be a relatively easy assignment because I had been working and teaching in the field for over a generation. I set out to draft a straightforward management book about how to transform organizations toward being more *dharmic* - that is, more honest and more spiritual. But the deeper I dove into the ocean of questions facing managers (and any working person) these days, the more profound the issues were. Ultimately, I found myself plunged into the big questions of life that people of all kinds (not only business people) are increasingly asking: Is what I do in life of any value? How can my life be more fulfilling? How might I live a life of more integrity, more wholeness - a life more attuned to what's truly important to me? What **is** life all about, anyway?

Those were deep questions, far beyond what I was prepared to write. I began to lose confidence and turned inward to seek help. Within a few days, Baba called me into His interview room and out of the blue assured me that I already possessed or would receive everything I needed to write the book. Emboldened, I launched into the writing and made substantial headway. But problems of self-trust didn't just disappear. At several points during the writing, I bogged down as I tried to explain particularly knotty issues. At one of these times, Baba again called me in. "You sometimes waver, wondering whether your writing is correct or if I will approve," He said, slowly shaking His head. Then He leaned closer. "**Your** inner voice is **me**," He intoned seriously.

I'm not so egotistical to think that He - this loving, small, brown man - was simply telling me that He agreed with what

I was writing. Something far deeper and higher was being communicated. He was telling me (and this applies to all of us) to follow inner truth. He was imparting the great truth that real Truth - capital-T Truth - resides in **us**. And He was saying that this inner Truth is God! - no less than that! He was also teaching that we have to learn to listen to that inner Truth and live by it.

I also soon discovered that any talk of spirit in business without addressing the issue of integrity in business is incomplete. Spirituality and dharma are inseparable. You can't, if you think about it, decide to be a more moral person without spiraling inward to considerations of what it is that gives rise to human morality (i.e., spirit). We may try, in our fiercely secularized Westernized societies, to divorce morality from spirituality, but sooner or later we begin to see that they are the same thing. To paraphrase Bhagavan's educational philosophy and apply it here: The real end of business is not profits, it's character.

The next three years writing the book was a wondrously blessed *sadhana*. Bhagavan, my beloved mother-father, took me strongly by the hand and led me through those swamps of low confidence and past the barricades of ignorance and shyness. "**Your** inner voice is **me**" continued to echo in me and bring strength. As I traveled this amazingly grace-full path, I was made to see that for today's managers and leaders and everyone else (because everyone nowadays is a member of some sort of organization), the key questions are no longer about task and structure but about spirit, integrity, and human values. The book became a humble presentation of Swamiji's clear truths about the erosion of spirit and the pattern of thoughtless dishonesty that is sweeping the world these days.

During those years of writing, it gradually dawned on me that this assignment was part of Bhagavan Sri Sathya Sai Baba's clarion call to dharma. This call is for everybody, for all persons in all walks of life, at all times, in all situations. And people who know Baba know that whenever He says anything,

He "means business" - in both senses of the word: he's serious about His mission to restore dharma to the world, and He fully intends to restore it in the business world as well.

And yet too many business people don't seem to be hearing this divine wake-up call. They seem to forget or ignore this important spiritual directive, or they simply don't think about issues of spirit and integrity. That's an important perspective - people just **don't think** about these things. "Business is business," they say, "and business has nothing to do with spirituality." They behave as though the moral standards we live by in life don't apply to business. "Almost anything goes," they say. They seem to take it for granted that the norms of honesty and integrity we use in life are justifiably bent out of shape when applied to commerce. When they think about it, of course, they see that this bending is not right. But, alas, they almost never seriously think about it.

Nowadays, more and more people are carrying those big questions about life values and life fulfillment with them into the workplace. They're beginning to see that living a more meaningful life at work requires facing up not only to spiritual issues, but also to questions of personal and organizational integrity.

In my book, *Reawakening the Spirit in Work: The Power of Dharmic Management,* "I" (Swamiji, really) explain that the word *dharma* is Sanskrit for deep, deep integrity - having the courage and self-discipline to live by your inner truth. I also explain that dharmic management means bringing that truth with you when you go to work every day. Dharmic management is the fusing of spirit, character, human values, and decency in the workplace and in life as a whole.

At one point, I reached out to a group of business managers for their straightforward comments about character in work. We talked for several hours about the competitive world out there and how one has to maneuver for position or get left out. They complained about the explosion of greed in the world and spoke of kickbacks and double-dealings that are so common in certain places that people think it's natural. They fussed about being forced into all this by "the system."

"That's the way it works," was their thin excuse for the lack of integrity and character in business. "It's the pattern," they said, their voices tinged with resignation and sorrow. "Take, take, take - after a while taking becomes second nature. Giving? Ha! You never even think about it." (There is that "don't think" again.) They summed up their woes: "Fact is, you have to make a living, and to do that, you have to be in an organization, and to be in one without self-destructing, whether as a manager or as a worker, you have to compromise yourself. Personal integrity gets sanded away. You erode your principles every day so you can live to erode them another day. After a while, you stop thinking about it, and the numbness helps somewhat." But that wee voice inside won't let them forget. "Man's conscience will always tell him," says Sai Baba.

I had asked them to shed light on the subject and was a bit surprised when they directed the glare smack in my face. Suddenly, somewhat dismayed, we found ourselves squinting at the harsh realities of life suffered by people in organizations.

Their comments can be distilled down to a few heart-rending queries:

- How do we live a dharmic life in a world that tears at our integrity?

- How can we scrub away the deceit and self-interest that sticks to us in organizations?

- How do we guard our values in this hard real world?

- How do we harden ourselves against compromise?

- How can we stop sandpapering truth?

- How can we overcome this widespread selfishness and greed that we are (actively or passively) victims of?

These are beastly questions forced upon us by the powerful demons that Swami tells us are devouring us: ego, greed, desire, anger, fear, and deceit. This is where spirituality enters. There is simply no way that we mere mortals can win against such monstrous adversaries. We have to enlist the aid of a power mightier than these demons; we have to turn toward spirit. We must heed Bhagavan's teaching to "always, **always** turn Godward."

In one part of the book, inspired by Baba's teachings, I developed some prescriptions for building character. They relate to the workplace but bear on all of life. Here are the edicts that pertain here:

*First of all, **think** about it.*

It's not simply that people are dishonest, and it's not simply that they are nonspiritual. In fact, it's just the opposite. People are honest inside and basically spiritual. A major part of the problem is that they don't ponder issues of honesty and have lost touch with their innate spirit and inborn goodness. They just never give it much thought, and they live in a society that doesn't give it much thought, and they work in human systems that don't provide support for living a more pure life. They're members of organizations that, passively or actively, contaminate people. People accept half-truths as just part of the game, and thus they condone them. And now, of course, they have a dim (or glaring) disquiet about the value and meaning of life.

A significant part of the remedy is simply to *think* about it! Thinking is the first step toward realization and awareness. Thinking about it is a definite act, a turning in the right direction. Once we begin contemplating these matters, instructions begin to flow to us.

*Be in the word, not of the world.*

Although we have to act out our parts in this worldly drama, we must not succumb to the dishonesty that exists throughout the world. We can, and must, play our roles with utmost reverence for dharma.

*Listen to your inner voice.*

Through thick and thin, remain attached to your inner truth. This is your direct line to and from your higher self, your personal connection with Source. Indeed, "Truth **is** God," states Baba. Living by our inner truth is what dharma is about. When people hear that, they take a quick breath and lean forward, their eyebrows arched: "You mean it may be possible for me to actually live by my inner truth?" The question may be more wishful thinking than a real question, but I answer it anyway, "Not only possible. It's imperative!"

*Develop your own life "credo."*

The greatest decisions of life are made daily in the silent inner garden of the soul. We must cultivate and nurture that private place. Writing up a personal credo, a manifesto of dharma, of integrity and character, is a way to further this. The credo can be used as a staunch life policy, as a personal constitution, as no less than a private covenant with God to guide our every act.

*Do no harm.*

Above all else, hurt no one. Sometimes, to get things done, it may seem that we have to bend certain rules. The point, as Bhagavan points out, is to never, ever go so far that it harms others or yourself. Never step even a little beyond your own sense of rightness because that sense is inner truth signaling.

*Put a ceiling on desires.*

Most people nowadays suffer from the disease of "more" (more material things, more status, power, prestige, etc., etc.). As carriers of this deadly ailment, we have to get serious about Baba's injunction to limit desires. We know by now that **more** is never enough! All desires, including even satisfied ones, just add lust for more! This malady is hatched from desire, which is one of those powerful demons. Turning toward spirit is the only way to fight it.

I'm reminded of a guest lecture given at Swami's university by an eminent economist. Speaking carefully in his British public-school accent, he lamented the dire, bordering-on-fatal condition of the world's economy due to rampant greed. Searching for a cure, he turned to Bhagavan's "Ceiling on Desires" program. Pausing for a moment, he slowly wagged his head as though in disbelief at the elegant simplicity of it. "It's so uncomplicated it almost slips past," he said, "but limiting desires is the solution. Economists may refer to it as 'demand management' or something that sounds more complicated, but ceiling on desires *is* the answer!"

*Empower purity.*

When you feel contaminated in work or in life, you have to scrub-up, and the sooner the better, even if it isn't being caused by a major circumstance. Contamination doesn't just sit, it accumulates. You're always becoming either cleaner or dirtier. The way to empower one's purity is keep it always in mind, to constantly think of it. Sounds simple, but it's true. When we continuously place our attention on something, it grows stronger. When we think constantly of our own purification, we become purer.

Bringing pureness so clearly into consciousness makes that the strongest part of us. Rather than continuing to suffer our dishonesty, we become beneficiaries of our purity. What's more, we can make it happen automatically. Steadily focusing on our innate purity each time we feel we're being corrupted not only helps us ride through the bad situation, it also becomes a habit. It's a form of mental reprogramming. Purity, after a while, is actually triggered by the intrusion of its opposite, and thus purity becomes self-enacting. It's just the opposite of thoughtless dishonesty.

This, of course, is the same mechanism as *namasmarana*, repeating the name of the Lord, which Swami prescribes for all of us. This wonderfully simple act actually brings the Lord and installs Him in our heart, and thus transforms our life. We can do the same with purity, installing purity in our being and transforming the foulness that inevitably comes our way.

*Regrow wholeness.*

Swamiji tells us to give ourself to Him. This means that no matter how bad our past mistakes, we can give them over to Him. Whatever it is that we lost along the way - heart, courage, purity - we can, with the help of spirit, grow it back. Slowly and surely we have to reclaim, refill, and become whole - and thus regain our true self.

The main task of the dharmic leader is to make integrity workable in the organization. An environment saturated with integrity soaks those who inhabit it in integrity. Coming to an organization already awash in integrity makes personal integrity easier. Good leadership creates the conditions in which people are always keeping what Swami calls "good company."

The dharmic leader does this three ways. First, he or she takes the lead in practicing integrity. Swami says, "As is the ruler, so are the subjects." The leader has to model personal integrity and then has to demand it. There is no other way. The moral character of an organization is leader-bound. The leader is either part of the solution or part of the problem. And yet this applies to everybody. People below the official top who aren't in a position of leadership must also take the lead toward dharma. You can't wait for higher-ups to do it. Each person in an organization is at the "top" of their own particular segment of it (even if it comprises only oneself). Character is **always** worked from the top down, and individuals have to take responsibility for their own actions from their own personal "top" down to themselves.

Secondly, the dharmic leader brings character to the organization by being crystal clear about his or her own basic values and the organization's values. The leader with character sends crisp signals: "This, by God, is what we stand for!"

Thirdly, the leader of character takes as the primary task of leadership nothing less than conferring integrity. It sounds audacious at first, **conferring** right action or simply **bestowing** goodness onto a human system. And yet the leader has to assume that this can indeed be done and that it is his or her responsibility to assign character.

You have to **endow** your people with the heart and grit to live by integrity. You literally **"in-courage"** them. You veritably **grant** fearlessness. You resolutely **require** self-discipline. You **expect**, adamantly and openly, that the organization lives by its collective inner truth. This is spiritual leadership. This is dharmic leadership as Bhagavan would have us practice it.

All of these tasks may appear to be new responsibilities for managers, leaders, and others in organizations. That's because people haven't thought about it much yet. But they will. And when they think about it, they will see that this is yet another facet of Swami's mission to feed the roots of integrity in the world. When people think about it, they will hear this as another note in Bhagavan's clarion call to dharma, and they will feel the rightness of it in their hearts.

(Adapted from material that appeared in "Sanathana Sarathi" and from Hawley's book *Reawakening the Spirit In Work: The Power of Dharmic Management*, published in the U.S.A. by Berrett-Koehler, San Francisco; in India by Tata McGraw-Hill, New Delhi.)

*"Dharma cannot be restricted to any particular society or nation, for it is closely bound up with the fortunes of the entire living world. It is a flame of light that can never be extinguished. It is untrammelled in its beneficent action."*

Sathya Sai Baba

# FROM DREAM TO REALITY
Deepa Awal

During our sojourn on Earth, much of what we wish for comes true. However, our dreams are desires that God, in His graciousness and infinite compassion, fulfills. Not only does He fulfill these human dreams, but He adds another dimension to them: He presents to us the possibility of dreaming the impossible, of attaining the unattainable. He brings to our attention a realm of existence that is beyond our ordinary vision, and He makes us aspire for that with an urgency we have never experienced before. This is an ordinary story of common dreams and desires made extraordinary by the grace of my beloved guru, Sri Sathya Sai Baba.

I was born and brought up in India, in a middle-class family. My parents were not especially religious, but they had faith in God, worked hard, and made a home that was both loving and supportive. They believed in a good education for their children and had high expectations of us. As the older of two children, I had always been encouraged to strive for my goals and to realize my potential. In my childhood, I remember, I wanted to join the Indian Administrative Service, a competitive and male-dominated government agency dedicated to administering the affairs of the nation and serving the people. My years in school and college were marked by several academic successes and scholarships, due largely to my father's encouragement and support.

By the time I finished my undergraduate studies in India, I was clear about my next step: I wanted to pursue graduate studies in the field of management and do something meaningful! I had many goals and ambitions, not the least of which was to be recognized as being bright, intelligent, and hardworking. The following years as a young adult were marked by several new experiences, including a traditional

Indian wedding, graduate studies, and my first job. In 1976, we moved to the United States, and a new era began in our lives.

For me, the move to America implied an opportunity for growth at all levels. I was looking forward to widening my professional knowledge and deepening my personal growth with the exposure to a new culture. Intuitively I felt this was the best thing that could have happened to me. In retrospect, I was absolutely right! Not only did I realize my dream, but I also realized that my dream was just a dream!

The first five years in the U.S. were intense both from a personal and professional viewpoint. I was raising two young children, working on a Ph.D., and working part-time. In those five years, I fulfilled many desires and ambitions. In fact, the personal and professional growth was so rapid that by the end of this period, I felt I was close to accomplishing much of what I desired. I had a doctoral degree in management and a consulting position with a leading multinational corporation. I had a network of professional colleagues who valued my work. I developed skills in the field of training and development and taught at a business school.

However, instead of feeling satisfied, I felt as if there were a vacuum in my life. All my accomplishments had failed to provide me with satisfaction or a feeling of completeness. Now it became crystal clear to me that happiness was not a function of accomplishments. There arose a deep yearning in me for gaining peace and for understanding the meaning of life. If I were asked to identify the one thing that was predominant in my psyche at that point in time, I would say it was a hunger for food for the soul. I was asking for an expansion of my being, my consciousness, and I did not know how to go about it or whom to ask for help.

It was at this time that Sai Baba entered my life. A few months earlier, a friend had visited Puttaparthi to see Baba. I had been greatly interested in her experiences. She invited me to a Sai *bhajan*, and I decided to go. It was just a group of people singing devotional songs, but the deep impact it had on me can only be described as a Sai miracle. I experienced a sense of homecoming and an emotional outpouring of tears that left no doubt in my mind that this was a relationship I had to pursue. Within months of that experience, I arrived in Puttaparthi to 'see' Baba. The visit was just for a day, but it started a relationship that changed everything in my life.

I returned to New York and picked up the strands of my life. The visit to Baba seemed to have had no perceptible effects on the surface, but in reality everything had changed. In the inner realms of my being, I began to accept Sai Baba as my teacher, my guru. I had no idea what this would mean, but I was willing to learn. It was the first time I had felt drawn to accept someone as guru. The faith, love, and surrender were still to develop, but a relationship had definitely begun, and the power of this extraordinary teacher soon started to manifest itself.

A change began to come over me. Life continued to promise the fulfillment of my dreams, for I continued to have a successful career, but now the dream had changed! I began to experience an intense restlessness with my life. There arose a desire for inner peace instead of outer progress. I wished to create a better environment in the home so that the children could experience harmony and peace, and I wished, above all, to be at peace myself. It was almost as if, without my knowing, a force was pushing me to re-evaluate my goals and reconsider my priorities. I had no choice in the matter.

One of Sai Baba's qualities is that He prompts us to see our desires and conflicts clearly and uncompromisingly. Sure enough, suddenly I had to confront myself as I had never done before. I could not deny my feelings any more. I had a growing realization that unless and until I was willing to let go of my earlier goals and priorities, there was no way of realizing new ones. I felt I had to completely let go of my professional aspirations to be able to realize inner peace and create the right environment at home.

The conflict generated as a result of these emerging new priorities was tremendous. I valued my work, the recognition, the network of colleagues and, last but not least, the financial independence. I was afraid that if I gave up all this, I would be lost. Yet I could not ignore the pressure of the inner restlessness and the certain knowing that something had to change. A part of me was urging me to release my external commitments and focus on myself and the home; another part of me was loathe to give up my status as a professionally active individual. The conflict lasted well over two years. In the initial stages, I ignored the inner struggle, explaining it as something every working mother feels at one time or another. But as time went on, I knew I could not ignore it any more: the inner restlessness slowly, almost imperceptibly, had gained force.

During this period, I asked Baba what to do. The answer never came clearly because there was so much confusion in my mind. The conflict grew in intensity until I could not hold it in any more, and I started to discuss the possibility of a part-time commitment with my partners. They were quite open to my needs. However, even this arrangement was not able to quell my restlessness. Now I understand why. In retrospect, it is clear to me that this intense emotional upheaval was the pain one experiences in letting go of the old and embracing the new. I was being forced to re-evaluate my beliefs and assumptions. The financial security, the status, the power, the independence and the recognition from the world outside were things I was dependent on for my self-image. Like most people, I let my self-worth be determined by what others thought of me. And here I was being prompted to drop all of this and discover my self-worth from within! However, I had no choice; the inner restlessness haunted me until I took the plunge. I quit, unconditionally.

As soon as this decision was made, a peace descended on me of a quality I had not known before. I was suddenly free to nurture my inner self and devote my time and energy to the children. I felt this was most important to me at that time. I had no regrets about my decision. In fact, there was a sense of freedom, both physical and mental. I was immensely grateful that I had had the courage to let go of existing ways of being and to reach out for new ones.

Life changed a great deal once I stopped working. It was like one phase of my life had ended and another begun. There was much more time for reading Swami's books, for reflection, and for reciting Swami's name. During the next few years, my life revolved completely around the children and Sai activities. It was a time for personal growth but in a totally different direction. The emphasis shifted from developing skills and abilities in the corporate world to understanding my own self: my motivation and purpose in life. This period brought about a tremendous change in how I saw myself. I started basing my self-worth not on how professionally successful and talented I was but on how I felt inside.

I discovered things about myself I didn't even know existed. For example, I started to see the value inherent in the culture I came from and how it had contributed to my own personality. I was more willing to recognize and act according to my own innate nature. Swami's teachings began to provide the basis for understanding human values and inculcating these values in myself and the children. I also tasted the sweetness of doing service in Swami's name, an experience I had never had before.

The few years that followed can best be described as safe, familiar, and physically easier. I plunged into discovering the world of house and family fully and completely. The resistance to full-time housework slowly dwindled as I tried to do every small thing with love and enthusiasm. I constantly reminded myself of Swami's words that no job is small enough to not deserve full attention. I overcame my notions of "uninteresting" work and focused on Swami and His teachings as I did the dishes and cleaned the home.

Looking back, I can see that while this period had its advantages, it also had certain disadvantages. As a spiritual aspirant, I began to think that withdrawing from the external world was essential for spiritual progress. This view is justified to some extent: just as a new sapling needs protection for its growth until it is strong enough to protect itself, a person new to the spiritual path needs to be watchful of the many distractions in everyday life and to focus on the essential pursuit of reality. But isolation is not the answer because it is life situations and people who provide the input for our growth and expansion.

Work is still an integral part of my life. Sai Center activities fill the day, but with a difference. I work not to earn money, but because it is my joy and privilege to do so. I delight in the people I meet, and am grateful for all they teach me. Never has work been so fulfilling as now.

Swami says the world is a reflection of Him. If so, the situations and circumstances we are given to deal with in our lifetime must be perfect for teaching us the lessons we need to learn for our evolution. It is in our interactions with the world that we discover our own beliefs, our own preferences, our own desires. Liberation cannot come until we let go of these. Letting go at the mental level finally implies loosening our preferences, likes and dislikes, at the level of action as well. If we really have no likes and dislikes, we are truly free. Understanding this more fully now, I realize the truth of Swami's words, "Life is a game, play it."

It has been 14 years now since Baba came into my life. Much has happened since then and the journey continues at a relentless pace. Many dreams are dissolving, and the ultimate dream of discovering my own reality is now the most potent. I am learning to look within for peace, love, and happiness. In an interview recently, I said to Baba, "The mind is very restless sometimes." He replied, "Peace is inside, not outside." This message has been manifesting itself in different ways in my life since the day I first set eyes on Baba. The conflict generated several years ago in the dual role as a professional and homemaker was but the first act in the play. Since then, He has unerringly hit the same mark again and again in many different ways. The message is the same: *Peace is inside, not outside.*

Much has changed. My criteria for evaluating and judging my life now are not what others say, think or feel about me, but who and what I feel I am. I am still ambitious but for different reasons. The ambitions I have for myself now are: Am I consistent in thought, word, and deed? Am I true to my higher self? Am I willing to be aware of my desires and expectations and let go of them? Am I willing to make my life simple so I can focus totally and completely on what is real? Am I willing to make life situations my teacher and learn fully and completely from them? This inner focus has opened up an altogether new world that is very rich and exciting.

Sometimes events happen externally and bring with them a totally new way of looking at the world. Sometimes I notice an internal change in the way I normally think about things. For example, I remember once standing in the line at the canteen in Prasanthi Nilayam thinking to myself, "Detached? There's no way I'm going to get detached from the children. I don't even want to get rid of this attachment!" And yet just a few years later, I found myself praying to Swami to take away the pain of attachment and allow me to realize my own reality. Slowly, but surely, the master teacher, Sai Baba, has sown the seeds of detachment.

Another time, again in the canteen, a lady from behind jumped the line. I was angry and frustrated but felt helpless to do anything except point out to her that there was a line. After what seemed like an interminable wait, my turn finally came, and I was served and seated. Soon after I had sat down with my plate of food, I felt thirsty but was reluctant to get up after having stood in line for so long. I started eating. In a few minutes, I caught a glimpse of the lady who had jumped the line. She had apparently finished her meal. Before I could realize what was happening, she flashed before me with a glass of water that she placed in front of me. I was completely nonplussed! Not only did the frustration and anger melt away,

I was overcome by a strange emotion which can best be described as a mixture of remorse and gratitude. I had been so quick to evaluate and judge her, and now with this one act of hers, my perception had totally changed. How limited we are by our judgments and quick conclusions, I thought to myself. It was a powerful experiential lesson in why not to judge and evaluate people.

Both these instances have one thing in common: they prompted me to re-evaluate and brought about a shift in my whole way of thinking and being. The greatest joy now is to expand and grow in such a way that the seams that separate me from the rest of the world disappear and dissolve.

Swami says He can change anything if He wills it, but He does not do that. Why? Because any change brought about suddenly without our own understanding will not last. So instead He provides us with ample opportunities by way of life situations, relationships, and events to transform ourselves and come closer to Him while He waits patiently. This is His greatest gift to us - what we call grace. Once we become aware of this, the world begins to look and feel different. Events that seemed purposeless before take on meaning; thwarted desires and wishes become vehicles for learning new ways of looking at the same thing. When difficulties arise, their resolution is less important than the lessons inherent in them. My prayer to God now is let His will be done, not mine. Such is the nature of the inner journey: there is nowhere to go, no state to reach, except to see our own reality, our own Self, at all times. I thank the Lord a thousand times for starting me on this journey of love and joy and complete fulfillment.

# ALL IS GOD'S WORK
Philip Gosselin

I remember my grandfather asking me when I was five years old what I wanted to be when I grew up. Although I had been named at birth for the hero in *Great Expectations*, to his amusement I answered, "I want to be a garbage man." My family certainly had high expectations of me and always placed a high value on career. My mother often counseled about work, encouraging me in this or that possibility, although, like the physician admonished to "heal thyself," she had a hard time finding her own vocation.

When I was a child, *Careers* was the family's favorite game. However, by the time I entered college, the game wasn't helping. I was stumped as to my vocation.

In my senior year, after reading many books on yoga and meeting a variety of yogis, I decided that being a yogi was a true and worthwhile vocation that matched my awakening interest in spirituality.

This new potential identity was at the same time very attractive to my ego, which was enthralled by the exotic grandiosity of seeing myself as some special spiritual being. My Western image of the wandering *sadhu* also matched my frugal, even stingy, qualities. My hippie inclinations at this time were to be a casual wanderer who could hitchhike everywhere and sleep anywhere. So besides being drawn to the spiritual life of a yogi, I was also drawn culturally and emotionally toward that image.

In order to go to India, after college I drove a taxi to earn my way. That temporary career became even more temporary than I expected. In fact, it quickly ended when two young passengers in the back seat of my taxi held a knife to my throat and demanded money. Fortuitously, they were seen and pounced upon by two undercover policemen who jumped into the taxi. Luckily, I had earned enough to go to India.

Shortly thereafter, I traveled to the ashram of Sathya Sai Baba for the first time. After living at Baba's for one year, He granted me an interview in March 1972. Joining me were my mother, my sister, and my future brother-in-law.

At one point during the interview, Sai Baba materialized a moonstone ring for my mother. A Frenchman in the room gushed out, "Oooh, that's so beautiful! Will you make one for me?" Baba replied, "This is not a store." He pointed to a plastic ring on my finger that had a cheap picture of Swami and said, "This is for money." Pointing to my mother's ring, He said, "This is for love." I looked down and noted that underneath Baba's picture on my ring was His motto, "Work is worship. Duty is God."

After Baba gave many teachings and admonitions, my sister, Janet, shyly asked the big family question, "What kind of work, Swami?" We all listened with bated breath, for everyone in my family present in the interview room had been puzzled about appropriate future vocations. Baba answered, "All is God's work. Teaching, office, family."

During the interview, He said to my mother about me, "Give him hard physical labor. He thinks too much." Baba told me, "Yoga just temporary." I knew right away that Swami's words meant that I couldn't find refuge in an identity or self-perception as a hatha yogi. He added about me, "Running here and there; this is not my teaching."

My search for an occupation to provide an outer persona was something that Baba demolished both during this interview and over the future years through His various instructions and hints.

After returning from India and over the ten years following, it seemed as though the jobs that I received were indirect gifts from Baba. After telling acquaintances about Swami after my first India trip, I was unexpectedly offered a training scholarship and a teaching job at the Arica Institute in New York, which was a kind of New Age yoga commune.

One late winter day in 1972, I was enjoying skiing by myself. The lift line was very long. After a half hour in the line, I found myself paired with an older person whom I took to be a business man. I foolishly assumed he was therefore uninteresting and so avoided any conversation. After reaching the mountaintop, skiing down, and going through the lift line again, perhaps an hour had passed - and amazingly I was again paired up with this same fellow.

This time I decided to be more open to him. He asked right away what I was interested in. I didn't mention religion or spirituality. I thought it might scare this "typical" business man. Instead I said, "Psychology." My chairlift partner then said, "Do you know anything about *avatars*?" I gripped my seat tight at this very unexpected question. To my amazement, he told me about a co-worker who had just been to see Baba. This was quite a powerful coincidence, especially in those days when Baba was much less well known. I could feel the hand of Baba in this improbable encounter.

My chairlift partner's co-worker later became a fast friend as well as a key figure in starting Baba centers in the Connecticut area where I'd grown up. This incident was a powerful lesson in my stereotyping and in my foolish egotistical separatism. A major irony was that I later became a businessman myself as well as a psychologist.

In the early 1970s, I took short-term jobs in order to go back to India as often and for as long as possible. After my Arica job and following another trip to India in 1974, I took a job teaching at a small institute in southern California. I had met the founder of the institute at an interview with Baba earlier that year, and I was hired because of my Arica teaching experience.

After a short stint at that job, I moved back to the East Coast in the fall of 1974. I took a job as a parking lot attendant to earn enough money to return to see Baba in 1975. After several months at the job, one day I put a car into parking gear and went to move another car. To my horror, I saw that first car move across the lot and crash into another parked vehicle. Apparently, the transmission had popped into reverse. This car belonged to a high court judge in town. Thus ended my parking lot career. Amazingly, I had just enough money to go back to see Swami. I promptly returned to the ashram.

After eight months at Prasanthi Nilayam, I again returned to America. My next short career was as a nursery school teacher. My future wife, Margaret, had convinced me to work with her at a Montessori school. She was keen on getting married and had asked Baba about it in late 1975. I was not ready for such a big step, and Baba said no to the marriage. Upon questioning Swami further, He did say, however, that we could work together - which we did as teachers shortly after in New York City. Again my work life was tied to my relationship with Baba through His "permission" to take this teaching work.

While I was at Prasanthi Nilayam from March to December of 1975, I made the acquaintance of several Wall Street businessmen who were devotees. I went out to California in the summer of 1976 to attend a Sai Organization meeting in Los Angeles. Afterward I hitchhiked north from Los Angeles, planning to spend the rest of the summer in Montana at friends.' After going about 30 miles, I couldn't seem to get another ride. I felt I was supposed to turn around and go back. It was the only time I had ever felt that way, and when I went to the other side of the road, I got rides almost immediately to the L.A. airport. I flew right back to New York. A few days later, on an August Sunday in a hot and empty New York City, a Wall Street friend I'd met in India called me because I had expressed some interest in working on the Street. A famous Wall Streeter and a close associate of his had to make a sudden move from one Wall Street firm to another and needed an assistant who could start that day. He was so desperate that he was willing to take on someone with little experience. My new job was a sudden gift - perhaps from Baba? Having just been a nursery school teacher for six months, I was now on Wall Street. When asked, "What's the quickest way to God?" Baba has responded, "Learn to love my uncertainty." Certainly I was trying.

Although now it's a stereotype that baby-boomers move from long hair to pin-stripe suits, in 1976 this situation was quite unusual. Still new in my job, I was invited to a party on the Upper East Side of New York. When I asked what to wear, the host said, "Oh, just informal." With much of my wardrobe consisting of clothing from my India trips, I blithely wore a rough cotton shirt emblazoned with Sanskrit mantras, and found myself surrounded by people in blue blazers and club rep ties. I was out of place, but I liked to imagine that I was "Baba's man on Wall Street," put there by Baba. It felt in accord with my assumptions that the world is an illusion or the play of the Gods. Initially, I also enjoyed the humor of the situation. Yet the world of money and power was confusing to a would-be yogi. I went to India originally to transcend and be away from the world. Baba, however, placed me directly in a most materialistic and worldly position. Swami has said, "Be like the lotus blossoming in the mud but untouched by it." Unfortunately, I often felt neither blossoming nor untouched by my situation.

I spent my first several years with a fast-growing firm and found it all very exciting. I was very lucky in the beginning. At that time in the market, when even financial veterans were having difficulty, I seemed to be handed clients. Actually, I wasn't much of a salesman, I was more like an intellectual croupier, helping peoples' gambling with my educated guesses about risk factors.

Sometimes I would become confused as to whether I was supposed to be selling harder. That didn't feel quite right to me. I had little urge to get people to buy securities about which they were unenthusiastic and which might not be too secure. I was well aware of attitudes around me at work, such as one bit of advice I received, "You have to be a bit of a thief to succeed in this business." I had puzzled co-workers one time by saying I didn't care about the money (certainly only partly true). One office joke compared me to Mr. Clean or Supreme Court Justice Earl Warren. I was secretly pleased, although to my co-workers these names were insults about my naiveté or lack of aggressiveness.

I would sometimes forget that the financial work was a gift from Baba, and I would feel that I was the doer. I would occasionally get caught up in the illusion of having the power to make people wealthy or happy. As a result, my ego would rise and fall with market fluctuations.

Now that I had a "regular" career and had started a family, I could only go for short visits to see Swami, but I still had the occasion in the late 1970s to be spoken to by Baba. In His presence, I felt some shame about my work. In India, I would feel how inappropriate this type of work was for a devotee. Occasionally, I would receive words or looks from other devotees about what an unsuitable line of work I had. However, Baba, with His own particular sense of humor and impossible-to-decipher agenda, seemed to feel quite differently about my work. In 1978, He asked me what type of work I was doing. The word "stockbroker" came out in such a constricted whisper that He asked me again. When I got it out, He was all smiles, telling me, "Good!" When I tried to ask Him if I should be in another line of work, He blithely ignored my concern. Instead He directed me to focus my energy on *sadhana*, work in the Baba Organization, as well as on my present job.

A very difficult work period started in 1981 and continued for six years. I worked for one company that went spectacularly bankrupt. Two other firms I subsequently worked for also went through much turmoil, eventually going bankrupt several years after I left them.

In August 1982, my family was fortunate enough to get an interview with Sai. I was quite down about my work situation, feeling that I couldn't make money for clients or myself. When I saw Baba, I complained silently about my work situation. Baba responded verbally by saying, "You're worried about your work. Don't worry. You will see. Everything will be completely different soon. Very soon." It was a number of months later before I realized that the day Baba had said that to me was the exact bottom of the bear (down) market and the start of the roaring bull (up) market of the 1980s. The Baba I know, knows all, but, as with the Delphic Oracle, the people coming to Him seem to be able to make only partial use of His words: I hadn't had a clue as to what Baba had been referring. Further, I still couldn't seem to make any money, and I was feeling the pain of losing other people's money. My situation was reversed from the '70s. Now it seemed that everyone else was making money and I no longer could. My ego was starting to identify me as a failure. Even though He had shown me His omnipresence, I was unable to see God as the doer.

Swami says, "I am like the dhobi (an Indian laundry person). First I raise them way up over my head, then I bring them down hard. I repeat this again and again until they are clean and then I hang them out to dry." Now I can often see Baba's washing action on my ego, but at that time I couldn't.

I stumbled through another five years as a stockbroker, at the same time trying to go into other related fields. There were many promising leads that seemed to end nowhere. Before, work had come almost effortlessly, and now nothing came, even with much effort.

In 1984, at my last interview, Baba looked at me disdainfully saying, "He's worried about money, thinks too much about money." Then changing His tone with all the soothing sweetness that He can bring to words, He said to me, "Nooo. Don't worry about money." Looking off into space, Baba seemed to transform into a wide-eyed country bumpkin seeing in his mind's eye a giant mound of gold. He started murmuring, "A lot of money." Then He looked at me with great amazement and what looked like envy and said, "A lot of money coming." Then, again, staring off into space, He mumbled, trailing off, "Two months, two years..." I almost felt that I was a conspirator with the Lord and should have responded, "Let's split it!" I was very pleased, but I also realized that there had been something very comic about His performance, as though He had been burlesquing my foolishness.

Lots of money, of course, never came. However, something better came of what He told me. Now whenever I think of money, I often think about "A lot of money" and that playfully sweet and intimate association with Baba. Money has become a private joke with the Lord. This Swami, who can turn the sky into mud and the mud into sky, could change a person's inner or outer circumstance. However, His interest is not in making devotees rich but in making their hearts rich.

Many speculations cross my mind when I think back on my Wall Street career. I wonder if Baba was trying to teach me to be more extroverted. Perhaps He was trying to show me the illusory world of up and down, high and low, rich and poor. Perhaps He was trying to jar me out of some of my habits, or even concentrate and accelerate my karma, or keep me in one place for my own good. Of course, I really don't know, but I do believe that in His grace He had used my work concerns as a way of connecting me to Him. My work life became inextricably tied up in my relationship to Baba. Perhaps my work life was used by Swami as just another way of remembering Him.

In 1987, I left financial work. I am now doing work as a psychologist that I find more satisfying. Recently, in the bull market of the 1990s, a friend excitedly called me to come back as a stockbroker, offering me another job on Wall Street, but financial work seemed like a funny lesson learned long ago. I've received calls from younger devotees asking for advice in how to maintain the dharma while working on Wall Street. Unfortunately, I don't have much sage advice. I found that "the world" and its ethical dilemmas did get to me. However, it also was a great opportunity to see how that illusion could grab me. I wasn't quite the yogi that I had thought or hoped, but I became a lot lighter and freer of inflated views of myself.

Perhaps this story may be useful for those who think about Swami and who are worried that perhaps their work life doesn't fit their devotional life. Interestingly, Sai told a close friend (also a would-be yogi) in our 1972 interview to return to America and work in his family's tobacco business. Perhaps it's not what you do that's so important. Perhaps what's important is that God is remembered. Let us hope that we all find, in our own way, that all is God's work. May we all be able to turn our work into remembrance and worship.

*"Ideas, principles, laws, customs, codes, habits, actions - all are to be judged on the twin points of intention and consequence. Is the intention pure, is it born out of Love, is it based on Truth? Does it result in Peace? If yes, Dharma is enshrined in that action or law, custom or conduct."*

Sathya Sai Baba

# THE JOB REALM:
## A WORKSHOP TO REVEAL THE SOUL
Veena Sundararaman

"You're a professional consultant. Your department should be paying you for your lunch hour!" said the woman from Personnel in amazement. "And they shouldn't be asking you to submit timesheets. That's for support staff and others!" What she was saying was news to me, and I could feel my temper rising. For almost a year with this organization, I had religiously tried to keep track of every hour that I put into or took off from work. If I was ever doubtful, I usually erred on the safe side and claimed less money. Swami lays importance on earning one's living honestly, and I didn't want to take any chances with *karma*. This care was also important since I was working at home and needed to establish my credibility with the organization. And here she was telling me that the department that had hired me had been paying me for one hour less each day than was common practice, plus my bosses seemed to be questioning my integrity by asking for timesheets!

Should I confront them? Should I quietly add all my previous lunch hours to my next timesheet? Should I forget the whole issue? The temptation to claim what was supposedly my money was great. But my conscience was not comfortable with the first two alternatives, and my ego wouldn't allow me to do the third. So I did what I usually do in such situations: I sat before the altar and prayed to Swami.

According to Dr. John Hislop in his book *My Baba and I*, when we have a problem about which we are uncertain or puzzled,

> *Baba says that we may be quiet for a while, think of him with all our intensity for 10 or 15 minutes, and then put our question to him. He assures us that before long our*

*mind will be clear, and we will know what is best to do.*

And Swami has also said:

*Since God is in every heart, the Inner Voice is the signal that Dharma gives while approving or disapproving any line of action. The Dharma you have to follow is indicated by that Voice.*

It is this perspective and this method, along with opening up Swami's books, that have guided all my soul searchings on *dharmic* challenges. The guidance I received in this case was that any pay I did not claim from the international development organization I worked for would be used for programs to help women and children, so I would be doing *seva* (service) by not claiming my lunch-hour pay. On the issue of time sheets, it was merely my ego being affected, and if I were truly honest in recording my hours worked, then I had no cause for anxiety. It became clear that Swami was thus ensuring that I was honest.

I have found that the inner guidance relays what is appropriate for each individual at a specific time. It may not be what we want to hear, but having asked, and knowing that the answer comes from a source higher than our mind, we have to follow it. The values may be tough to live by in this day and age, but we have chosen the resulting freedom as our goal. And the deep peace and joy that follow make the effort worthwhile.

I remember a study circle in a New York City Sai Center years ago where the topic was "ethics in the work place". I was greatly influenced by some of the thoughts shared, such as using office copy machines for personal copying was not right action. It made me start trying to apply Swami's standards to every action in the job sphere.

But right action stems from right attitude, right thinking and feeling. One time I got a job as a proofreader in a large investment firm. I had landed the job without the required experience, so I believed that Swami's grace was responsible and initially I was very happy. This elation soon turned sour when I found myself overqualified for the job. When every effort I made to show initiative and get above my position failed, depression set in and I was sorely tempted to quit. All my prayers indicated that I should not quit the job, that I would be removed when the time was right. Why would Swami want me to work in a position where I felt inferior? I asked myself constantly.

I stayed on for close to two years, during which time, to earn much-needed income, I had to humble my pride, curb my ambitions, and continue to do a sincere job, knowing all the time that I was capable of much more. I could not disobey my inner voice.

A few months after I had received inner guidance that Swami would move me from the job in His time, the company merged and most of the staff, including myself, was laid off. His grace had ensured that I would get money in the form of good severance while leaving a job in which I was not happy! Besides, the skills I learned in that job, such as attention to detail and accuracy, and the qualities I acquired, such as perseverance and patience, have been of enormous benefit to me ever since. I also learned the value of Swami's teaching that freedom lies in liking what one does rather than doing what one likes. Moreover, from His teachings and what He has told individuals in interviews, it appears that the kind of work one does is not as important as **how** one does it, with how much love one does it.

For me, the work sphere has been a battlefield. Swami says, "Everyone's heart is a Dharmakshetra where the battle between the forces of Good and Evil is fought." I have learned to pray intensely for His guidance and for the strength to listen carefully, to follow it, and to trust His will. While we are fighting the oft-hidden negative tendencies within ourselves, it is hard but important to remember that we are not "bad" and that each dilemma we face and struggle through removes a layer of our personality to reveal more of the wonderful, loving, pure, divine being that we are. The people He uses to teach us are illusionary, the themes are make-believe. It is His will that manifests itself. This thinking has helped me in many an agitating situation. It allows me to avoid blaming individuals for their actions and to see them as Swami's way of teaching me something. And with the Lord constantly guiding us, it becomes an exciting adventure.

For over three years, I worked for an international non-profit organization that was a cauldron of seething emotions and theatrics. Even outsiders would comment on how many "difficult" personalities and situations seemed to have come together under one umbrella. Once again, I was prevented from leaving this stressful environment by the intuitive feeling that this would not solve anything: the experiences would simply repeat themselves until I had learned what I was supposed to. Almost on a minute-to-minute basis, I was forced to think deeply about what was right for me at that moment and to be bold enough to take right action based on peace and detachment and faith in Swami's teaching that we are truly One. It was very difficult.

During that particular testing period, I saw others being given projects that I was keen on doing. Colleagues took on tasks that I considered in my scope of work. I began to realize that I needed to carefully scrutinize my motives and be sure they were pure before I proposed to take on any task, for desires of all kinds can lie deeply embedded in one's consciousness and pose as good intentions.

Once, even my job title was given away. After receiving the high-sounding designation, I had opened up a book of Swami's and found jumping out at me His words on the futility and emptiness of titles. He cautioned spiritual aspirants against getting attached to them. I'm so glad I took this timely warning seriously. Shortly thereafter, a new organizational chart was created in which my title was the only one removed!

"I set tests not as a punishment or because I enjoy putting

you into trouble, but just to give you the joy of passing," Swami reassures us. I often felt that I had failed. For every step I succeeded in, I fell several steps back. I often got dejected and felt I was not worth being called a devotee. But in His infinite compassion and divine understanding, Swami would invariably send my way a quote, a thought, or an experience to save me from such despair and encourage me to continue on the spiritual journey to my Self.

Sometimes self-inquiry might reveal that our persistence in a task is being tested; at other times, our levels of detachment and contentment are under scrutiny. In one job, I had been working on a project proposal for over a year. During this time, top management did not pay much attention to it. When it was finally ready for submission to funding agencies, however, the senior officers started to take a closer look, and suddenly the project became a high profile one. At this point, the CEO and his team decided it should be taken over by other staff. Having put in all the time and effort that I did, I was torn. My emotional self wanted to give in to feelings of hurt and anger at the superiors for depriving me of the opportunity to see the project to its successful completion. But my higher self realized that nothing happens without Swami's will. So instead of wasting time and energy in feeling hurt and angry, I decided to consult my inner "boss." Swami, within, guided me to unhesitatingly give up the project by giving me the understanding that it was better for me and the project this way.

Often I wonder if I am really hearing my inner voice or if my mind is playing games with me. My own experience has been that if I take a leap of faith, time shows me whether I was tuned in correctly or not. In either case I learn, and that is what is important. In the above situation, time revealed that on account of my subsequent ill health, the project would have strained me too much, and that asking people for money was best done by someone other than me. Swami knows the future, while we do not. If we try to follow His teachings and place full faith in Him to guide and protect us, it becomes increasingly easy to let go of attachments.

Our ego prevents us from realizing our divinity. I have learned that when we are at a crossroads where we have a tussle between divine consciousness and ego, we have to make a deliberate decision to sacrifice the ego and manifest divinity. Swami says, "Every single unselfish act which prepares the ground for the merging of the Soul with the Over-Soul, which broadens the vision towards the basic Brahman immanent everywhere, is a Dharmic act." It is not easy, but with Swami's grace and our effort, surely in time it will become our instinctive behavior.

An interesting experience I once had relates to the correct use of time. One year when I got seriously sick, one of my big worries was how I would put in a 40-hour work week when I had to spend about 15 to 18 hours a week in and around hospitals and also had limited energy. I needed the full-time status to get medical benefits. I prayed intensely to Swami. To my utter astonishment, I received inner guidance that the best course of action for me under the circumstances was that instead of going to the office, I should stay home three days a week, concentrate on God, and work to the best of my ability. I was to have utmost detachment from the results and not worry about the hours I put in. "Who would agree to such an arrangement?" I wondered. I was really taken aback when my office, as though in confirmation of this direction, started encouraging me to work at home as much as I needed to.

After about six months, my headquarters finally counted all the days and hours I had taken off. When I should have clearly run out of sick leave, their records "mistakenly" showed that I had more days left! My own boss thought their calculations were "bizarre." But I knew this was one more Sai *leela*. Lest this gives the impression that Swami encourages us to take it easy and get paid for it, what happened to me next will wipe out that illusion. As my health improved, the pressure from the office mounted for me to either make up hours or take a pay cut. Having gotten accustomed to my "custom arrangement" of flexible hours, I started rationalizing within about why this schedule should continue. Swami says:

*In all worldly activities, you should be careful not to wound propriety or the canons of good nature; you should not play false to the promptings of the Inner Voice; you should be prepared at all times to respect the appropriate dictates of conscience; you should watch your steps to see whether you are in someone else's way; you must be ever vigilant to discover the Truth behind all this scintillating variety. This is the entire duty of man, your dharma.*

When I prayed to Swami for His guidance, I saw very clearly that as my mind and body began to feel healthier, what was right action for me had changed. Earlier it had been appropriate for me to take time to rest and meditate. Now it was necessary for me to use that same time in working hard on my job. By forcing me to either put out more work or give up attachment to money and take a cut in pay, Swami was clearly protecting me from building negative karma. Once I accepted this divine teaching on karma and dharma, no one bothered me anymore. The situation was resolved by the organization proposing that I work a four-day week, take a pay cut accordingly, and still continue to receive full medical and other necessary benefits. In all the lessons I am exposed to, when I have faith that Swami has my best interest at heart and is watching over me with love, I find that He makes the best arrangements!

Implicit in this whole discussion of the work place is that our work must qualify as seva. The attitude of serving has to be the foundation for and permeate all our activities, particularly in the job sphere, where we spend so many hours of our day. Swami says:

*By saturating the service with love, work can be transformed into worship. When the work is offered to God, it gets sanctified into puja (worship). This makes it free from ego. It is also freed from the earthly desire for success and the earthly fear of failure. You feel that, when you have done the work as best as you can, your puja is accomplished. It is then for Him who has accepted the puja to confer on you what He considers best. This attitude will make the work unattached.*

I have found that trying to put these divine teachings into practice is the greatest challenge and yet brings the greatest joy. Doing work as selfless service is the only way to eventually disintegrate conflicts within oneself and with others, to be rid of all concern of approval and anxiety about results, and to generate love and harmony. Then our work can finally become true worship.

# MY BATTLE TO SURRENDER
## Jack Scher

I spent the last seven weeks with Swami, where He thrashed and trashed my tangled karma, unravelling the very fiber of my being, renewing all that I had learned to call "me." I know now that in order to follow my dharma, I must control my appetites and desires, accept all that happens, and surrender my will to His will. Above all, I must trust Baba completely, trust that He loves me. Then, basking in His light, I can be more loving to those around me.

In many ways, at age 67 I still act like a voracious, deprived child. My father died when I was 5, and my mother remarried when I was 8. Shortly thereafter, she was stricken with polio, which left her paralyzed from the waist down. My whole family was focused on my invalid mother's needs. There was just no time for me, no time for anyone to properly love and care for me. I grew up feeling deprived, angry, and rebellious. I felt like an indentured servant, as if I were there only to serve my mother's unrequited appetites. I was forced to look outside myself and the home for approval. As an adult, when I found the recognition I sought in a successful career in medical publishing, I thought that I alone had overcome life's trials, tests, and hardships. Little did I dream that all this time, God had had me under His wing, taking care of my every need.

I first came to Sai Baba in 1985. I was 58 years old and I thought that now, having retired, I was reaping the rewards of my own efforts and good fortune. When I learned of His words, "Not a blade of grass moves without My will," it was extremely difficult and even disappointing for me to accept the idea that God had made all my accomplishments possible. I had to erase the pride I had taken in my efforts, and I was fearful of losing the confidence I had earned from the battles I thought I had won; my sense of personal satisfaction from my perceived achievements was at stake. Giving all this up meant having to learn to accept the concept that, at the very least, my success was due to the miraculous combination of His grace and my efforts.

One of my greatest challenges has been to understand the doctrine that I am not the doer, as well as to accept and live by that doctrine. For me, there seems to be a paradox surrounding the concept that everything is His will and yet it takes a **combination** of His grace and our personal effort to make things happen, as Baba says very emphatically.

I am beginning to realize that this partnership, or wedding, between effort and grace actually occurs on some other level. For instance, how does having an interview with Baba come about? First, you have to be in Prasanthi Nilayam. Do you get there because you choose it or because He has brought you there? Baba says that no one comes to Him unless He calls them. Let's skip that hurdle and assume that you are there. Only Swami Himself will decide whether to come over to where you are sitting. Did He or did you choose where you would be sitting?

Whenever He comes toward me, I strain to catch His eye, to plead and appeal to Him for attention. But, again, does He motivate me to move like a puppet on a string, as I reach up poised with a letter hoping to embrace Him with my adoration? We think we have to do something, when in fact all He wants is our love; He says that as the Lord of the Universe, He has everything else.

On one miraculous day, He stopped and asked, "Where are you from?" and my heart leapt into my mouth. It took an enormous effort to say "Virginia." What part in that play did I have? My Lord Sai Baba stood before me in all His glory, and He and He alone *chooses*! I must remember this, for my very sanity; I must give up thinking that I have any role in this selection.

In the past, I have bathed and dressed carefully, hoping in some way to appeal to and attract the Lord. Now I see that I must bathe and dress carefully out of love and respect, but not to attract Him. He would be attracted by nothing less than an open, loving heart. If I can only accept that He and He alone is the doer! What a tremendous relief it would be to surrender and accept totally that all is His divine will.

As I breathe deeply, enjoying the embrace of His protection, my monkey mind goes back to work, asking about my partnership with the Lord of the Universe. I know that my dharma is to do my duty, to perform every act with the right motivation. I must trust my heart and not my mind. I have been taught that desire and attachments are the traps that lead to anger and sorrow, that true surrender to His will is the royal road to happiness. Yet I keep coming back to the question of how and when I am to do my share to keep my part of the bargain. I now know that He writes the script and He is both the producer and the director, but how and when am I to act in His play? What is my role? When, if ever, do I come on stage? True, I am just a puppet, but if I am required to put forth an effort, how do I find out when and how to fit into His drama? I know that I am not supposed to just sit back and expect that Swami will take care of everything. Yet as soon as I say that, I know that *He does and will take care of everything.* To put it plain and simple, when and how do I make an effort?

My habits and the way I solve problems are very deeply ingrained. For most of my adult life, I worked or fought my own way to the top, or so I thought. The motto on my graduation ring from New York University was "Prestare Est Prestarus" (To persevere is to succeed). In spite of my rebellious attitudes, I accepted this rule, even lived by it. Whenever I felt insecure or undeserving, I worked harder, believing that if I put out my best effort, I could assume my victories were well earned.

Because hard work seemed to deliver, I became dependent on it. My trust centered upon mobilizing everything I had to plan creatively, and then to follow through relentlessly until my goal was achieved. I played the game like any businessman, overlooking small slips in personal morality to win the prize.

However, in spite of my enormous drive to overcome my childhood deprivation, I never once was ruthless, nor did I ever purposely hurt anyone.

Anticipation was a central source of pleasure for me. I would enjoy planning how to win almost as much as the victory itself. Even in my personal life, the dream of how and what I would be doing was sometimes more delicious than the actual experience. I enjoyed living part of my life in the future. The important thing was that my modus operandi worked; I trusted and depended on my proven methods. Now, with Swami, all of a sudden I was learning that my entire approach to problem-solving was wrong. I realized I was not really responsible for my success and that I owed it all to Him, to God!

When I am sitting at Swami's feet at Puttaparthi, it is not too difficult to accept that God does it all, especially when He seems to be showering me with His grace, but when I am back home I can easily forget this. It is terribly hard to break old habits, especially when they have worked so well. I remember the first time I came to Puttaparthi, sitting day in and day out, week in and week out, feeling acutely the deep pains of personal rejection. Each day Swami would walk by and seemingly ignore or look through me. I was the invisible man bemoaning my fate. Nothing I did helped. It was clear all was in His hands but, at that time, I only had an inkling that He and only He controlled everything.

Slowly, I began to realize that I was suffering so much because I refused to give up my old techniques for winning. He was grinding me down, bringing me to my knees, teaching me that *anticipation is a killer*. I had to let go. At darshan, I would put my head down when He was still on the women's side and begin to pray, "Baba, please just smile or stop or say something, please show me that You love and accept me. I will give up everything, I will surrender all my desires for an interview, just for Your smile." My dream was for me to be sitting there with my head down and suddenly to feel His gentle hand touch the top of my head, and then to look down and see the bottom of His brilliant orange robe, His small feet poised directly in front of me. Well, it never worked. All my self-control and discipline vanished as I sensed Him approaching; my past training and dependence on expectations was too hard to throw off. Almost against my will, I would find my head rising and I would cautiously look in His direction. Then I would get caught in the throes of desire, and my dream would collapse.

On my first trip, I made eliminating anticipation and desire my mantra. Over and over I would silently repeat, "Anticipation does not work, anticipation is harmful, anticipation causes pain, anticipation is the mother of desire. Desire is the all-consuming tragedy in my life, I must eliminate desire, I must be empty to be free." There were many variations, but the theme was the same: eliminate anticipation and desire - and surrender. During this first trip, I began to understand these truths, but I didn't realize they were just the tip of the iceberg. The real task lay before me.

On many subsequent trips, I would eventually discover and realize that is was *doership* that was the culprit. It is only now, after 10 years and 11 trips to Swami, experiencing His love and His relentless lessons, that I am just starting to know and accept that He and He alone is the doer. If I had surrendered earlier, I would have felt like I was relinquishing my life. Now I am starting to see that my real life and purpose for existence is just beginning.

On my most recent trip, on the very last day, I went outside the ashram to purchase a few more Baba photographs to possibly use for the covers of some of the Sai books we were publishing. I selected about 10 photos from two shops on Chitravatri Road. They were all 7 inches by 10 inches. However, at the last minute, a larger picture caught my eye. It was too large to fit in the shopkeeper's paper bag, so I rolled it up gently and went back inside for bhajans.

In between darshan and bhajans, Swami decided to walk around, taking letters, chatting with His students. As He moved in my direction, the thought occurred to me that perhaps if I held up the photo with my pen clipped to the top, He might decide to stop and give me the unbelievable joy of signing the photo. As He came closer, I cautiously held up the photo, silently pleading in my heart, "Swami, please sign this. We are leaving tomorrow." At that very moment, He stopped, turned and looked over toward me. I was sitting about eight rows back from Him. My prayer was that He would signal me to come forward. Instead, looking straight at me, He said, "When do you leave?" I said, "Tomorrow," and He started to walk forward towards me. The sea of men in front of me parted, so He was able to walk up to me directly, smile, and lovingly sign the picture. Tears of joy clouded my eyes as I gratefully looked up and lovingly touched His foot. My love and gratitude knew no bounds.

Rejoicing now as I stroke the loving memory of this event, I dare to ask myself, what role did I play? Where was my personal effort? True, I went out and purchased the pictures, but who chose that photo too big to fit in the shopkeeper's bag? Who or what force motivated me while sitting so far back in a sea of men to hold up the picture and ask for His grace to sign it? Only *He*, the Lord of the Universe, deigned to answer my prayer. He bestows His tender, loving grace when and where He chooses. The joy that came when He stopped and graced my picture with His signature was His to give and mine to receive. My role in His play was to be there and to know, accept, and understand that He put me there. Whatever outward actions I took were in response to Him. The sooner I accept and understand that He and He alone is the doer, the sooner will I find my own peace and happiness.

I surrender all at His feet. My part of the bargain in this game of effort and grace is to keep the doors to my heart open, to act with love as my motivation, to appear at times to be a partner in the doing but to know deep down inside that He and only He is the doer, and to celebrate my total surrender to His will.

Yet how do you hold on to that clarity and remain calm and composed when the whole world seems to be rigged against you? For example, our departure plan was to take the morning flight from Puttaparthi directly to Bombay right after darshan. This way we would avoid the long and tiring taxi ride to Bangalore and avoid worries that the mid-day flight from Bangalore to Bombay would be canceled. We would arrive in Bombay just about noon, with lots of time to rest in a hotel, shop for a few last-minute gifts, and arrive well-rested for the 11 p.m. check-in for our flight to Rome. Instead our plane from Puttaparthi was grounded in Coimbatore, an out-of-the-way stopover on our flight to Bombay. We were told there was a problem with the hydraulic system and a replacement part was on its way from Bangalore. It was not yet 10 a.m., and I was still floating in a blissful state from the morning darshan. Besides, we were in Swami's hands, what could go wrong? By noon I was getting a little less complacent; the news from the check-in counter was the replacement part was due any minute and the repairs would be completed in half an hour.

Sometime after 1 p.m. I began to feel that it was necessary for me to investigate further and to see if this was one of those times for me to exercise the *effort* part of my partnership with God. Sure enough, the duty officer told me the plane would be grounded until the next morning and that all the flights from Bangalore to Bombay were fully booked and wait-listed. At this point, I temporarily forgot my training and my faith that Swami would take care of everything. I pleaded with the duty officer to get us on the next flight to Bangalore, which was scheduled to depart in 10 minutes.

Baba was with us! The officer agreed to change our tickets. We ran across the tarmac, waving at a luggage tractor carrying our four bags, hoping they would get our bags on the plane to Bangalore. Breathlessly we boarded, and in 40 minutes we were in Bangalore, an hour too late for the midday flight. We begged and cajoled and most of all prayed at the different airline counters, but there just were no seats available for the last flights of the day to Bombay. Our best hope was Indian Airlines, where the duty officer said he would try to get us moved up on the waiting list because of our need to connect to an international flight.

I was totally exhausted; my patience and forbearance were nowhere to be found. My only thought was, how could we be sure to get on the Bombay flight? I thought I would try to offer the duty officer a bribe. I knew this was wrong, but I felt desperate. I see now that I had completely lost my belief that everything is His will. In spite of all those lessons and my insights into the underlying principles of this game of life, I was trapped again into thinking that I was the doer. My wife, Judy, was horrified at my suggestion that we attempt to bribe the officer. She reminded me of the many painful lessons I had just learned, of how the way we act is more important than the end result. She said that I was now, hopefully, spiritually clean; it was unthinkable to consider offering a bribe. Immediately, I knew she was right, and I just sat there in the airport lounge, ashamed that I had even considered such a thing. Mind you, I have no experience in bribing, but I did feel terribly let down and fearful that we would miss our flight to Rome.

At 3 p.m., we were told to return at 6:30 p.m. to see if our wait-list position was cleared. We considered going into town for a few hours, but I was too anxious. Finally, I realized that we had to surrender to this, and I began to try to find some of the trust in Swami that had somehow vaporized. Judy went over and asked the duty officer if he would help us store our bags in a safe place so that we could go into Bangalore for a few hours. He smiled and said he would be glad to help. For some unknown reason, Judy said ever so gently, "It would be so nice if you could sign the ticket over now." Although she had asked him to do this several times in the last hour, somehow this time the man simply said, "Yes," and dutifully signed the magic letters OK on the tickets. I almost cried with relief. Swami had been there all the time. I had just lost my way and could not remember how to find Him.

Our flight to Bombay took off on time and we were in the international airport by 10:30 p.m. We were not well-rested, as we had planned earlier, but we were terribly grateful as we boarded our 2 a.m. flight.

On the plane, too worn out to sleep, I quietly wondered why Baba wanted me to have this tumultuous exit. Was it to remind me that without Him life is unbearable? Did He create these painful trials to keep me focused on Him? Or were these difficulties just more tests to see if I had really learned the lessons I had so proudly proclaimed I knew and understood? Was the purpose of this hardship to get me to remember what I had learned? If I had had an easy departure and slipped right back into my worldly life, I may have forgotten these lessons. Or, suppose it was a miracle. Baba decided to save our lives. He knew that if the plane to Bombay took off it would crash due to a defective part, so He made the technicians aware of the fault and saved us. Perhaps it was just His way of keeping me close to Him, because He knows how adversity makes us turn to Him, at least when we have the wisdom to know and remember that *He* is the doer.

Whether this was a miracle or not, I was more than a bit disappointed that I failed my first test so miserably. There was no excuse; to think that I considered bribing the duty officer showed how little faith I had in the Lord, and since I am part of Him, how little I had thought of myself. I had not yet learned that all is His grace and that I must surrender to whatever He has in store for me. I thought I had resolved to surrender, to know that I am not the doer, and to trust that all is His will. He quickly taught me that I have a great deal more work to do, that aside from understanding with my head, I must begin to understand with my heart if I am going to live in this new and wonderful way.

I am still very shaky from this experience. I am no longer proud that I know the truth and have found important answers to life, but rather I am humbled by the task in front of me. I now know that the first thing I must do when things seem to

go wrong is to sit down, take a deep breath, and pray to
Swami. In spite of what will take enormous effort and resolve
on my part, I am determined now to follow my dharma and
really trust that He is the doer, not I!

Two weeks after that trip home, I awoke suddenly in the
middle of the night. It was as if a veil that hid my ability to
see the truth had been removed. I lay there, all my previous
conceptions shattered by my mind's clarity. I immediately
understood why I had struggled so hard in my battle to
surrender and accept that all is His will: I dreaded giving up a
far greater attachment that was the very underpinning of my
existence.

I had refused to admit that I do not have *free will.* I see now
that my struggle with His doership was a paper tiger to keep
my real terror at bay. I was feebly attempting to deny the
obvious: *We Do Not Have Free Will.* For years I had read
everything I could find on what Baba has said about free will.
There was always an element of doubt until that moment that
allowed me to hide the truth from myself. I desperately wanted
free will in order to avoid feeling powerless and without
control. It was as if I were fighting for my very life. I needed
free will to justify right and wrong, good and bad, praise and
blame, karma, and last but not least, why we are rewarded
when we are productive. Now I have to give up these grandiose
pretensions.

The real test of dharma comes when we know that we have
no free will and yet we are still responsible for our actions, that
we readily accept His doership and yet we also embrace His
basic rule that everything that happens is the result of the
combination of His grace and our efforts. So we still have a
paradoxical partnership where we must do our duty, where we
must do our very best. We must act as if we had free will, and
yet know, trust, and love that all is His will.

It was at this point that Baba, knowing what I needed to hear,
led me to page 101 in the book *Dreams and Realities, Face to
Face with God.* The author, Dr. Bhatia, tells how he pleaded,

"Baba, please withdraw this free will which You have given to human beings." Bhatia prayed for an answer to his question. On Baba's birthday, Swami motioned him to take padnamaskar, but Bhatia refused and continued to pray for the answer to his query regarding free will. "Swami lovingly patted me on my back and said the following words that will always echo in my ears: **'Bangaru, nothing is free will, everything is My will.'"**

Now, I am beginning to glimpse what I really am - His glorious instrument. My sole purpose in being is to find my own path to my own Divinity. Service is the route I have chosen. I will love and serve my fellow man and through them, hopefully, I will find Him inside myself. I see now that in the end, our final surrender is really to ourselves. Only when I can face the fact that ultimately we have no free will, will I be able to relinquish the battle and finally begin to surrender.

*"Whoever subdues his egoism, conquers his selfish desires, destroys his bestial feelings and impulses and gives up the natural tendency to regard the body as the self, he is surely on the path of Dharma; he knows that the goal of Dharma is the merging of the wave in the sea, the merging of the self in the Over-self."*

Sathya Sai Baba

## CHEERING ME HOME
### Sheila Firnstein

Growing up as an Orthodox Jew made me feel separate from the world. Eventually, because of this and my longing to explore a life with less restrictions, I left Judaism behind. Years later, I was guided back to my roots through my profound connection with Sathya Sai Baba and His teachings. Reconciling these two seemingly diverse paths is the greatest dharmic challenge of my life.

The journey began when I was born in an Orthodox Jewish family, the youngest of three children. We lived in a middle-class New York suburb by the ocean in a community of observant Jews. Dad was the pillar of the community, raising funds for the synagogue and religious schools and frequently taking leadership roles. He was handsome, charismatic, and controlling. Mom was incredibly loving and giving to us and to all who needed her attention.

The community was an extended family. Both of my parents came from large families, and we were constantly surrounded by aunts, uncles, grandparents, cousins, and friends. My maternal grandfather died before my birth, so my grandmother, Bubba Celia as we called her, spent the years of her old age between the homes of her seven daughters. She lived more than 100 years, giving us all the opportunity to experience the benefits of three generations living together. She could not have stood more than 4'8" tall, and yet we all secretly referred to her as "the general." Her sage advice to my parents saved my adolescent neck many a time, as when mini-skirts became the rage and my skirts went higher and higher. "It's all right,'" she would say in Yiddish. "Leave her be, this is what they wear now. You want she should be different?"

My paternal grandparents lived around the corner from us, and I would frequently visit them on my way home from school. Bubba Chanku would always welcome me with smiles, hugs, and a tasty pastry to eat. But it was my grandfather, Reb Menashe, who intrigued me and drew me there. As he heard my footsteps on the stairs, he would clap his hands in delight, chanting my Hebrew name over and over in his deep, gruff voice, swaying back and forth as if praying. All this just to welcome me! Reb Menashe was a deeply religious man, the mystic of the family. His long, scraggly grey beard and sensitive hands are etched in my memory, as are his eyes, which were inscrutable. He must have softened considerably as he aged, for we heard tales of his iron-fisted discipline with his own children.

He had moved his family to America from Czechoslovakia in the 1920s, leaving behind his two eldest sons, my father and my uncle, so they might continue their studies, for he didn't yet know or trust religious education in the new country. The boys were treated poorly, and my father suffered severe illnesses and feelings of abandonment during this time of loneliness, for he was very attached to his mother, and he blamed his father for taking her away. Dad joined his family in the States by the time he was 16 and was always a model son and brother. However, the part of Him that remained the abandoned little boy would surface whenever he felt hurt by someone. He would withdraw in anger and become unreachable, and his heart would close down to the offender. Unfortunately, all three of us, his children, learned this behavior all too well. I believe this was what caused our family to abandon each other later in our lives.

For the most part, my memories of our way of life and the celebration of our religion are joyous and rich - from tender moments saying my bedtime prayers with my father to the grand and holy moments of Yom Kippur, watching my parents pray to God with tears of intention, sincerity, and devotion. They inspired in me a deep appreciation of the importance of prayer, ritual, and community. To be so loved and connected is a great and wonderful thing, yet if one fears the loss of such love, it can shape one's choices and one's life, as it has mine.

As a child, I felt somehow different, perhaps as an immigrant might still feel apart and separate even after learning the language and customs of a new country. Maybe it was my natural perversity, my strong desire to be an individual, for I was headstrong and willful, yet firmly connected to God in a personal and direct relationship, speaking to Him as if he were an older friend or guide. For some reason, I never perceived God as punishing. From an early age, I desired a more liberal path for myself than that of my parents. I felt separate from the greater world of "real life" that I viewed only through television and the movies, and I longed to be part of it. On the Sabbath, when I was not allowed to watch television, I read voraciously of other people, other times, and places.

Because all my important life choices were influenced by the laws of Orthodox Judaism and our culture's pressure to conform to a certain standard, my imagination became my only escape. I was sent to the same religious day school from kindergarten through high school, and my little rebellions seemed a necessary part of remaining an individual. I ditched school when I could, smoked cigarettes secretly, and argued endlessly, especially with certain teachers who irritated me with their dogmatic style of teaching Jewish laws and customs. "Why," I asked, "must I observe custom as if it is law when it is not?" This was not an idle intellectual exercise, for my life was dictated by these religious decisions. The answer I received was always a variation on the same theme - that Judaism had survived thousands of years and has remained intact due to a series of "fences" built around the laws in order to protect and preserve them. If each individual chose what to observe and how to observe it, by the next generation we would have something very different than the Judaism that has been given to us. Very few people I knew chose to leave the tradition, and certainly no one that I knew chose to intermarry, for that provoked the most severe penalty of all - ostracism from family and community. Custom required such families to ritually mourn that child as if dead. Although I did hear of one or two cases in other communities, I knew of no one personally who chose such a fate. Indeed, my friends seemed satisfied to remain within the bosom of family and community.

Although I yearned to go away to college, my father would not allow it. I commuted daily to a city college. At 18, I was offered a "dream job," but it required my working on the Sabbath, so I had to turn it down. For the same reason, I let go of my desire for a career in theater and television production. At 20, I did what was expected of me: I married a good-looking man from our community. Although I had the new status of wife, it became apparent quickly that I had no more freedom in this environment than I had had in my parents' house. As my husband was controlling and I still rebellious, the marriage lasted only three years, but it produced my only child, a son, Brett.

On my own with my baby, I began to explore my freedom for the first time. Freedom from all rules, especially religious, was intoxicating. It wasn't long before I began seeing an old summer camp sweetheart who had broken away from orthodoxy. He was living in California, completing his Ph.D. in psychology. After two years of a long-distance romance, Brett and I moved to California to be with him. My father was very angry and barely spoke to me as we said goodbye at the airport. I remember asking Him if he was angry because my new partner was not religious or because we would be living together without being married. He claimed the latter, but I knew he was heartsick at my abandonment of religion. Before too long, we did indeed marry and my family welcomed my new husband with open arms. My mother had never stopped praying for our return to our heritage, believing we could never be happy so cut off from our God and our people. Mom knew me better than I knew myself, for she knew I was deeply spiritual.

I spent a number of years basking in my freedom but never really felt at home in Southern California. I found it difficult to replace the loving friendships of a lifetime, and I missed my family very much. I came to realize that my husband was truly an atheist, and I began to search for spirituality outside of religious doctrine. I took classes in yoga and began to meditate, beginning to explore my inner self.

One evening in the late 1970s, I entered my yoga teacher's house and noticed a new photograph on the mantel. Something drew me to the picture of a small dark man with a large Afro hairdo wearing an orange gown. Although I had never seen such a person, I felt a familiarity. I can remember my exact thought as I looked at Sathya Sai Baba's sweet face for the first time: "So this is who you are." Strangely, I did not dwell on this thought or pursue it. I felt calm and relieved. I just accepted my inner knowledge of this Indian holy man. He began to appear in my meditations as a loving, supportive force and guide.

Shortly thereafter, my teacher left for India to see Baba. At the time, I had no desire to go there. The thought actually horrified me.

Since my husband did not support my interest in spirituality, I felt I could not possibly pursue my connection to Baba comfortably. I eventually stopped meditating and tried to become part of the local community. I opened a business and reached out for more friendship, but emptiness grew inside of me, some terrible yearning for something deeper, for a sense of belonging. I felt lost in a wasteland of material values and friendships that kept slipping away. My husband and I drifted apart.

During that period, the best time for me was when my family would visit. To prepare for their arrival, I would scrub the kitchen from top to bottom, put all of our regular dishes away, and unpack my kosher dishes, both meat and dairy, conscious to follow all the Jewish dietary laws so my family would be comfortable in my home. We always had a good time together. Brett loved being surrounded by the warmth of family, and he loved the richness of the ritual they brought to our otherwise secular environment: my dad rising early each morning to pray, wrapping himself in *tallit* (prayer shawl) and *tefillin* (phylacteries), my mom lighting the Sabbath candles to create a holy environment. These were profound moments.

Later, when my mother was diagnosed with metastatic breast cancer that had invaded the bone, we rallied close around her. She tried all the medical treatments offered, including an experimental drug that killed off all the cancer but left her to bleed to death. It horrified us to witness the cruelty of the illness compounded by the effects of medical intervention. Totally bereft, we could hardly believe that Mom was gone. Her unconditional love had buttressed and unified us, and after the initial period of mourning and mutual support, the very structure of our family shook with strife. Within a year, my father remarried and I divorced, each of us feeling angry and abandoned.

Feeling empty and desperate, I collapsed in tears and begged God for joy and fulfillment. Within days I met Paul, the partner I had been waiting for all my life. We met at a dinner party in a restaurant. Although I noticed Him immediately, it was he who sensed something deep between us and pursued the relationship. Perhaps the reason I did not recognize Him as my "soulmate" was because he was not Jewish. I had never dated a non-Jew before. I wanted the common background on which to build a relationship, just as a common native tongue facilitates communication and intimacy. But Paul would not be discouraged. His love was so sincere that I felt I was coming home to my very self. Once united, we found the joy, the sense of wholeness for which we had both been yearning.

I knew my family would not be happy that I was dating a non-Jew, but I knew they loved me, and I expected that they would accept us when they saw how happy I was. Or perhaps I needed to believe this in order to move forward with Paul. Before long, both my father and brother came to California to reason with me and to warn me that if I should marry Paul, according to Jewish law, I would be cut off from my family, my people, and my inheritance. I knew this was the custom and recalled hearing of families that had actually "sat shivah" (ritually mourned) for the loss of the loved one to intermarriage. My father refused to meet Paul.

Paul and I never talked seriously about his conversion to Judaism because I knew the only conversion that would be acceptable to my family would demand Paul's commitment to live as an observant Jew, something I myself was not willing to do. Paul had been raised as a Catholic in a predominately Italian city in upstate New York, and interestingly, as he carries a German surname, he was consistently misidentified as a Jew. As an adult, he has had many Jewish friends and business partners. His being drawn to me certainly fit this pattern.

Paul liked to think of himself as a Jew and, to confuse matters even more, he often wore a Jewish star. However, I knew that in Jewish tradition, we do not encourage conversion. It is a soul decision that one must pursue and be persistent in order to obtain. I took this seriously, never encouraging him. Besides, when Paul observed the severity of my dad's response, he did not want to be a part of anything that caused so much pain. He felt responsible and guilty for coming between us. As our relationship deepened, so did the pressure we felt. We rarely talked of marriage since the only ritual that was meaningful to me was within Judaism and with my family's support.

Eventually, Paul and I took off for six months of travel in Europe, for we needed to be on our own to discover whether we were truly well-mated or simply standing strong together against the storm of disapproval. I left Brett, then 12 years old, with his stepfather, with whom he was very close. My family refused to see me or take my calls. I felt cast off and set adrift, on the one hand, and well-anchored by the most important relationship in my life, on the other. During that time, pain became a constant companion of my days, and frequent nightmares assailed my nights. I knew my family was also suffering, and I must admit I took some satisfaction in that, for how, in the face of such love, could they cut me off so mercilessly? It has been my perception that inherent in orthodoxy is a deep and resounding belief that theirs is "the way," given by God. My family stood firm, never questioning their rightness. I could rationalize all of this mentally, but emotionally I was hurt and angry.

My father continued to refuse contact with me. I gave up, carrying the misery of the rejected daughter with me wherever I went. Paul and I decided that our best strategy was to move as far away from the pain as possible. When an opportunity to live in Australia surfaced and Brett expressed a desire to join us, we jumped at the chance to create new lives. On departure, with the angst of new beginnings facing us, a friend gave me a small photograph of Sathya Sai Baba to light our way. I was happy to receive the little picture and tucked it away in my wallet.

We arrived in Sydney hopeful, frightened, and feeling a great sense of responsibility to Brett, who was entering high school. We found a townhouse in Paddington and a non-denominational Jewish school with excellent teachers and small classes for individualized attention. I hoped Brett would connect with his heritage in a balanced way, as the focus was on culture rather than religion.

However, the stress built quickly as Paul and I worked hard to earn a living and tried to cope with an angry adolescent who was deeply hurt and confused by years of feeling abandoned by us and who was now in a strange environment without family or friends. We all tried our best but felt overwhelmed by our emotions. My deep feelings of guilt and remorse only complicated the issue more. Some nights, it felt like we had come home to war.

In desperation, I reached back into meditation as a drowning person grasps at a lifeline. For a meditation place, Paul had painted our little spare room a rosy lilac color that lifted me and created a feeling of clarity. I looked around the house for holy objects or pictures to focus the energy and found none. Suddenly, I remembered the little photograph of Baba tucked away in my wallet and, having no suitable frame, I propped it against an existing hook on the wall. "Baba," I said aloud, "I am ready to know you now. We need your help very much. As a first step, we need to meet some of your people here. But please send us people like ourselves who are not too pious so we can relate to them." Since I hadn't thought about it before, the spontaneity of my request rather startled me.

Two days later as I arrived at work, a man I didn't know came up to me and handed me a beautiful yellow rose. I carried it with me, stopping at a secretary's desk to drop some papers off. In the course of conversation, I mentioned I had just begun meditating again after a long hiatus in order to deal with my stress. Her response grabbed my attention. "I have these friends you might like to meet. They go to India to see an avatar." Without hesitation, I asked, "Sathya Sai Baba?" She was more stunned than I, for at that time I did not know what an avatar was.

The next day she brought me two books and suggested that Paul and I read them before we meet her friends. I was already sensing Baba's guiding hand and responsiveness. It was with a great deal of excitement and hunger for knowledge that I read *Man of Miracles* by Howard Murphet and *The Holy Man and the Psychiatrist* by Dr. Samuel Sandweiss. Within days, Paul and I had consumed both books and were eager for more.

On the following Thursday, we stood before a strange house. I smoked a last cigarette before going in, convinced that spiritual people didn't smoke. As we entered, we were greeted by a cloud of cigarette smoke - the two women of the house smoking my brand. (I know now that Baba discourages such habits, but at the time it was the perfect environment for me to relax in and be myself.) It was important we feel right at home because the sights that awaited us as we entered the meditation room were unusual, to say the least. The room was filled with pictures of Baba and saints from many traditions. Many of the pictures were covered with a thick ash that filled the room with a special fragrance and a distinctive heightened energy. We had read about this ash, called *vibhuti,* but nothing we read prepared us for seeing with our own eyes the miracle of manifestation. We heard story after story of incredible miracles and healings and found out that the vibhuti had first begun to manifest in this house on the day of our arrival in Sydney nine months earlier. These new friends were zany and filled with fun, yet serious about Baba and their spiritual development. They became perfect escorts for our first trip to Baba.

India seemed like another planet, so vastly different were the sights, smells, and sounds. A new awareness began to unfold even before we reached Baba's ashram in Puttaparthi. We felt anticipation and excitement building in us, along with some anxiety. What would it feel like to be in the presence of a being we believed to have unlimited consciousness? We did not sleep the night before the final leg of our journey.

On our first day at the ashram, in the oppressive heat of the Indian summer, we rushed to prepare ourselves for *darshan* (to be in the presence of a holy being). My first glimpse of Baba as He emerged from the *mandir* (temple) confirmed my inner picture of him, for He was beautiful and graceful as He glided ever so slowly in our direction. In his radiant aliveness, I could almost see in the light that seemed to emanate from Him the beginning of His aura. Then He stopped, and it looked like He was writing on an invisible blackboard. He turned His head and spoke a few words to what appeared to be empty space. In those fleeting moments, I wondered with distress if we had come this long way to meet a madman. Baba resumed a slow and concentrated movement toward us, smiling at one person and whispering sweetly to another. He stopped nearby, and His right hand made a downward spiral as He produced a fine ash that He delivered into a waiting hand. As I watched His retreating back, awhirl with conflicting thoughts and emotions, I felt as if He were still watching us, sensing our reactions. I was totally overwhelmed as I realized He was far more than I could ever know.

Although I was continually surrounded by many people, my internal dialogue quieted. I had no thoughts of the world outside of the ashram. In that stillness, I began conversing with Baba from the deepest recesses of my being, as if I had internalized him, for indeed, eyes opened or closed, I could see Him imprinted indelibly just behind my eyes. On the last day, I climbed the hill behind the ashram and found a seat on the wall overlooking it to bid farewell and have a parting conversation with Baba. I let myself feel the sorrow and hopelessness of the separation from my father. It was at this moment that I received what I can only describe as a transmission, a thought as clear as day, implanted in me: "**You are here with me by the grace of your father's devotion to God.**" Stunned, I focused my awareness, as thoughts changed to flashing pictures that seemed to bypass my mind in order to communicate with my soul. I can only say that I was shown the interconnectedness of all and the infinite possibilities for resolution through love. For the first time in years, I felt optimism as I walked away armed with a plan to meditate each day, visualizing my father as a small child that I would hold, rock, and comfort.

At home, I continued the visualization daily, and when I felt a subtle shift occur, I wrote to my father telling Him that I was planning a trip to the States and that when I arrived I would call with the hope of seeing him. I also stated that I would understand if he could not see me. Months later, I stood at the door of my childhood home, my brother at my side for support, and rang the doorbell. After five long years of separation, my father opened the door to receive me. We chose our topics of conversation with care to stay on safe ground, but after that day, I felt free to call and stay in touch.

I saw Him once more, at my brother's birthday party. I stood before Him unexpectedly, and as he looked up and saw me, his face was unguarded. His eyes lit up with the joy of seeing someone he loved. That memory sustains me.

I was never to see Him again. Dad died suddenly two weeks before our scheduled move back to the States. Grief-stricken, I flew home, leaving Paul behind to close up our house. Our parting was painful, as if saying goodbye to each other and the friends we had made were ripping apart our cocoon. I was afraid to go home to New York and be confronted by the reality of my loss. I dreaded the possible reaction of my family and community who all knew "my story."

In Judaism, after the funeral, we mourn initially for a seven-day period called *shivah* (which literally means seven). It is the time for the immediate family to grieve and receive support. Friends and family bring food and serve the bereaved, and all who know them come by to offer comfort. It is an amazing healing practice and a sane manner of dealing with loss. The last time I had stayed in our house was for my mother's shivah eight years before.

All through shivah, I allowed my feelings to flow unhampered, supported by family and friends and rooted in ritual. At the same time, Baba felt as close to me as my own breath, like the Kashmiri shawl I wrapped myself in.

We had been at Baba's ashram shortly before this. By then it had become apparent to me that Baba's method of teaching differed for each individual. I discovered His method of choice for me is to direct me within to find the guru residing within my own self. Although I felt His powerful guidance and constant awareness of me, He often gave concrete attention, such as personal interviews and gifts, to my friends. (I churn even now out of gratitude, on the one hand, for the incredible grace He has bestowed upon me and out of my desire, on the other hand, to "have it all." Perhaps as a daughter who has felt rejected by her father, it may be unrealistic for me to expect to be without desire when it comes to wanting recognition and acceptance from Swami.) Finally, I began to perceive that events that occur when I am with Baba are really metaphors for situations that unfurl and confront me in life. Baba, as my master instructor, began preparing and grooming me for the future by weaving a tapestry of people and events to teach me a critical lesson.

I was feeling pretty good, having made peace with my father and thinking I had truly learned my lessons on rejection. One day I was sitting outside the mandir writing in my journal when I recognized the cadence of Australian accents in a conversation behind me. I turned to the woman closest to me and told her I had lived in Sydney, and as she did as well, she asked which Sai center we attended. When I told her we did not belong to an official Sai center, she lost all interest in me and turned back to her conversation. I felt discounted, and that old, familiar sense of being different, being wrong, was quickly followed by a feeling of strong dislike for this woman. Just then Baba appeared on the veranda and gave me a long look, which I believe set my lesson in motion. At the time, this seemed like a small event, but I see now that this is my pattern. When I feel rejected, I reject. From then on, I ignored this woman whenever she crossed my path, which strangely happened all too frequently for the next few days.

At the next darshan, Baba called a couple we knew and the woman's young daughter for an interview. I watched with interest as the three of them were seated on the veranda of the mandir waiting for Baba to lead them into the interview room. Then, to my amazement, Baba stood before the woman and motioned for her to leave. As she walked away through the seated crowd, I could not help but project my own feelings of rejection and humiliation on to her. Later, Paul and I discussed what we had witnessed. We agreed to respect their privacy and ask nothing about the interview or the seeming rejection.

However, when we ran into the man in the village about an hour later, he clearly wanted to share his interview experience with us. He told us that Swami seemed to want Him to get married. He was shocked by this because Baba had received Him and his woman friend as a couple several times before, never questioning their relationship. As the man handed each of us a packet of vibhuti Baba had given out during the interview, he asked us not to repeat this information to anyone. Paul and I were stunned and confused. We knew none of this was a coincidence. Of course Baba knew we were not married.

A moment later, still grasping the vibhuti packets, we found ourselves alone on the street as a car approached. Paul whispered in disbelief, "It's Baba's car. He's in the back seat." Paul, feeling somewhat guilty, dropped back, while I stepped forward waving and calling, wanting to make the most of this unexpected opportunity for one-on-one darshan. As the car drove slowly by, Baba gave me a steady look, then with a resolute movement of His head, He turned away from me to face the empty ashram wall. I felt devastated. A lone figure followed Baba's car, and as I recognized the Australian woman, something broke loose inside of me. Pain and rage swept through me, as I agonized over Baba's apparent cruelty. I reasoned that if Baba knew we were not married, He must also know that I was in an impossible situation: if we married, I would alienate my family forever. Why was He confronting me with this issue?

I was relegated to the back lines at darshan. (Seating at darshan is chosen by lottery. We have witnessed that the law of probability does not seem to apply as, inexplicably, Baba seems to choose our seats.) I tried to close my heart to Baba and stewed in my misery, feeling neglected, unloved, and jealous of all on whom He lavished His loving attention. Over the next days, I slowly calmed down and began to observe my reactions and thoughts. I realized that a lifetime of feeling different and never living up to others' expectations had made me dislike myself: I only liked those who saw me in a good light. As I thought about this, I knew that Baba was reflecting back my own rejecting nature, my lightning-fast instinct to cut myself off from anyone who rejected or hurt me. I also realized Baba was showing us that the issue of our marriage was far from resolved.

Feeling more peaceful and kindly towards Baba, I realized I could choose a different response to this lesson. Even in the face of rejection, I could choose to remain loving and not choose to **be** rejected. As I was sitting outside of the mandir once again writing in my journal, the Australian woman sat down next to me. This time I greeted her eagerly, moving over to give her more space. When she heard I would be leaving for Sydney the following day, she asked if I would carry an important message for her friend. I agreed, and offered her the back page of my journal for her note. A moment later, Baba appeared on the veranda and glanced in our direction. This time I could feel His approval, and I knew that I had successfully completed this lesson.

I felt as if a pall had been lifted from me. Later, as I told Paul about the experience, I knew Baba would confirm my "graduation" by giving me my first front-line darshan. (Throughout three visits, I had never drawn a front-row seat.) I dressed carefully for this occasion and put a flower in my hair.

As sure as I had been, I was startled when my line actually went in first. As I sat in an extraordinary place directly across from the mandir, waves of emotion engulfed me - gratitude, love, and anticipation of this awesome darshan. Silently I begged Him not to come out until I had calmed myself and could benefit from the experience. As if Baba could hear me, He stepped out just as I was ready. This day, He did not follow His usual course: He bypassed a whole section of women to walk directly up to me. I was too stunned to speak as He stood before me gazing at me with great love. As He turned to move on, I finally managed to call out, "Swamiji." He returned to stand before me once again and, with incredible tenderness, He motioned gently with His right hand, Wait, wait, wait - His eyes so soft on mine, dark pools of compassion. He left a wide berth between himself and the other women as He headed toward the men's section. I had been the only woman that darshan to receive such grace. I felt fully confirmed in the completion of my silent lesson and more confidence in my internal process for the future. I felt acknowledged and loved by Baba, but a part of me felt a tremor of apprehension at all this attention. For what was I being prepared?

Three months later, I knew. Just after we completed sitting shivah for my father, I received a phone call from his attorney. He wanted to speak to me before the formal reading of the will. I had been disinherited.

Miraculously, my heart remained open as I accepted my father's decree and sought to understand his reasons. I learned that my father had written his will in secrecy at the time Paul and I had moved Brett to Australia. I surmise that he had realized then that we were committed to each other despite the fact that we had not married. He had fulfilled his obligation to Jewish law and, perhaps by doing so, he had freed himself to open to me once again. Had I been given the choice of his money or his heart, I would have chosen the latter.

After weeks of absorbing and working this through with my family, I flew to California to meet Paul, who had just purchased a comfortable old camper. We began a search for a new place to settle, travelling through the States to visit with family and friends and look for "our community." On one of our many trips, we drove through Oregon and stopped at the town of Ashland to visit some people we had met at the ashram. I can remember seeing the sign as we pulled off the freeway and remarking to Paul, "Ashland, like vibhuti-land. I wonder if this will be significant for us."

It was a Thursday when we arrived, the day when Sai groups often meet to sing devotional songs. We enjoyed these songs that evening in nearby Grants Pass. It gave me strength to be with Sai friends. As it turned out, much more awaited us that weekend. Our hosts in Ashland were Jewish Baba devotees. They had moved to Ashland after hearing of this small community being led by a rabbi that practiced a form of Judaism called "Jewish Renewal" that sought to be inclusive, to go beyond dogma to the heart of the tradition. Our hosts had become part of the Havuruh (a community of friends, from the Hebrew root word *haver*), and when they heard about my background, they encouraged us to stay for the Sabbath services.

Friday night, after lighting candles and having dinner, we walked to a little white church in town. From the moment I crossed the threshold, I had to fight to remain a neutral observer, for all of my old religious training came to mind and I began to judge a Jewish group that would meet in a church. This was nothing like the synagogues or the services of my youth, and yet in some ways it seemed much more. It felt as if the air itself were charged with awareness.

A group of 25 or 30 people gathered around the candles, singing a haunting melody that called to my soul. The rabbi accompanied them on guitar, his shoulders draped by a traditional black-and-white tallit, a small *kepah* (skull cap) bobby-pinned to his curly hair. One by one the candles were lit, as each person spoke a blessing from their heart. In the golden glow of the candles, a holy presence seemed to descend in the circle of open hearts and friendship. Joyous music followed to welcome the Sabbath, interspersed with traditional Friday night prayers. Everything was so different, yet deeply familiar.

The following morning at services, I felt totally unprepared when the rabbi called me up to the Torah and gestured for Paul to join us. In Orthodox Judaism, only Jewish **men** are called to the Torah. With Paul by my side, I recited the Torah blessings for the first time in my life, then followed the Hebrew letters inscribed on the parchment scrolls as the rabbi, reading from the Torah, chanted the ancient melody. I was overcome, feeling my soul powerfully connected to this form of worshiping God. The rabbi and the rest of the group gathered around us to bless us with raised hands. I could feel Swami's presence clearly.

I slipped away as soon as I could, needing to be alone to work through the quantum shifts that were taking place within me. My tears fell freely as I felt an overwhelming gratitude to Baba for understanding me better than I did myself and providing for my needs. He had indeed sent me back to my roots in a joyous way, to a community that was inclusive of Jews and non-Jews, men and women alike. Many in this group had searched elsewhere for spiritual growth and were bringing back their treasures, from Buddhism, Hinduism, and Native American traditions, just as I was bringing Baba with me.

We rented a house for the summer to have a closer look at Ashland and its intriguing Havuruh, and here we have remained these last four years except for several trips, including two visits to Baba.

Miraculous developments have occurred that have healed the past pain and separation. My brother and sister-in-law came for a visit and fell in love with Paul. Together we shared the Sabbath. Paul took on special chores with great joy, cleaning the kitchen as his contribution for the preparation of the Sabbath, a day of total rest, prayer, abundant good food, and time for family and friends.

The Havuruh has become our center. We celebrate and support each other through births, Bar and Bat Mitzvahs, weddings and deaths. In a small community, all hands are frequently needed, and we pitch in wherever we are needed, including the *Hevra Kadisha*, the group responsible for preparing the dead in a sensitive and conscious manner for burial according to the laws of Judaism. We have found our base for spiritual practice and feel it authentically "ours."

As we became more deeply involved in the community, Paul began to think of converting and, just as he had approached Baba carefully and slowly but with deepening love, devotion, and commitment, so he approached Judaism. Paul was not supportive of anything that could be seen as divisive, and therefore he refused to agree to any conversion that would not be recognized by **all** Jewish people. For this reason, he insisted on an Orthodox conversion. I truly believed this to be an impossibility, for why would an Orthodox rabbi agree to initiate someone who was not willing to be Orthodox? But as miracles have a way of ironing out the details, my brother took up Paul's banner, contacting an Orthodox rabbi in New York.

He told the rabbi all about us and Paul's deep involvement in Jewish community life and his desire for conversion. Interested, the rabbi called us and asked many questions about how we lived, how we celebrated Sabbath and the Jewish holidays. In the end, he was more than satisfied that Paul met the requirements. He said to us with great love and respect, "It sounds to me like it's Sabbath every day in your house. I would be honored to help you." Paul studied with our rabbi in Ashland who, as I, had been raised in an Orthodox home. Paul chose a Hebrew name, Ami Ram, that honors both of his chosen paths. In Hebrew Ami means "my people" and Ram "to be exalted." As Paul explained, he was making a commitment to the Jewish people as well as to God. I couldn't help but think Swami would be very pleased.

The conversion rituals were very simple yet profoundly moving. Three rabbis formed the necessary Jewish court, with my brother and son supporting Paul so tenderly and protectively. During the ritual immersion, I had been asked to wait outside in the hall for reasons of modesty, according to the religious standard. But suddenly I heard my name called, and I went forward. The rabbi's soft heart had given way as he understood our deep connection. Paul looked into my eyes as he said the blessings. None of us will ever forget the holiness of Paul's face at that moment, so vulnerable and pure.

Four days later, after being together for more than eleven years, Paul and I were married in a synagogue in New York. My father's tallit served as our wedding canopy, supported by my four nieces. I stood barefoot on rose petals collected by friends in Ashland, as we listened to a soul-stirring song by our dear friend, the rabbi from Ashland, with words from the Story of Ruth: "Where you go, I will go. Your people will be my people, your God, my God." My brother stood facing us holding the cup of sanctification, the very cup my father had held every Friday night. My brother united us with all of his blessings. I had come full circle.

As my body has two legs, so my path is grounded by Baba and Judaism. Judaism gives me my daily practice. I say blessings when I eat, drink, see a rainbow, hear a clap of thunder or receive news of a death. These disciplines serve to remind me constantly that there is a God. But it is Baba's presence in the world that gives me heart and the courage to explore who I am and how I can be. Each time I visit Baba, our internal conversation becomes more clear, and I am beginning to glimpse our unity. Since our most recent trip, I spend 24 hours a week in silence learning to listen more deeply to my own inner voice and to truly hear and receive others. Each morning, I prepare for the day by praying and meditating. As Baba says, "It is only in the depth of silence that the voice of God can be heard." And He says, "Prayer is speaking to God and meditation is listening to God." I am striving to achieve both sides of that conversation.

Although I am finding satisfaction in the integration of my paths, I am not so reckless as to believe that all Jews would applaud or support my path or my choices. As it happened, the rabbi who married us and converted Paul was not prejudiced against Eastern religion. Although he was unfamiliar with Baba, he listened with interest and an open mind. When he heard that Baba had sent us back to our roots, he said, "I'd like to meet Sai Baba." Perhaps he will some day.

As baggage from the past, I still carry distrust and an over-sensitivity when I feel I am not being accepted. Even now in our own community, we have friends who cannot understand the desire and need for Baba in our lives. I tend to be intimate with those who do understand and try not to close my heart to the others.

I struggle on, finding my voice as a Jew and as a Baba devotee. A few years ago, Paul and I were with Swami for Hanukkah, just after we had found Ashland and Jewish Renewal. Each day of Hanukkah, the festival of lights, I was fortunate enough to sit in the front row at darshan. At one darshan, Swami manifested vibhuti for me and a friend. On our most recent trip, I expected similar treatment, but Swami does not repeat himself, and this year's outward Hanukkah grace moved to Paul. My grace this time was given as teachings, what I came to think of as "illuminations" on major questions for each day of Hanukkah. Here is one from my journal:

"... a more subtle teaching from Swami about my practice of Judaism - not to let it separate me from others and not to live in a "ghetto" with it. One God, various styles of worship. The work is union with God, not separation from others. Perhaps this is why Paul has been given all the close darshans and other grace. Paul is beginning his journey as a Jew. I realize, had Swami given me this grace now, I would have grasped Judaism as my banner, rather than making it simply my practice. No good over-identifying and creating more attachment...I can also see Baba's wisdom in not giving me too much direct attention early on in our relationship. Had He done so, I would have grasped too closely to ever be able to embrace Judaism as well."

It is my dharma to be a Jew and a Sai devotee. I have been given a rich stew to savor and grow on. It is my task to find my way to unity. My life-long feeling of being different and separate is fading as I see that I fit in everywhere and nowhere. I now see the benefit of being able to move from culture to culture, sharing who I am, passing a message through my very being, for our lives are truly our messages. This is a great joy and an awesome responsibility.

> *There is only one caste,*
> *The caste of humanity.*
> *There is only one religion,*
> *The religion of love.*
> *There is only one language,*
> *The language of the heart.*
> *There is only one God,*
> *And He is omnipresent.*

*"Out of free will I have taken this human body for re-establishing dharma among all humanity. I shall not rest until my mission is finished. My life is my message."*

Sathya Sai Baba

# GLOSSARY

**Adharmic**: Not living by the dictates of God, doing your duty, or following codes of morality.

**Ananda**: Bliss.

**Arjuna**: White, pure, unblemished, unsullied; Arjuna was one of the Pandava brothers and the hero of the *Bhagavad Gita.*

**Asanas**: Physical postures.

**Atma**: The spark of God within, the soul.

**Avatar**: An incarnation of God, the descent of God on earth.

**Bhagavad Gita**: "The Song of God," a major Indian scripture.

**Bhagavan:** The Lord, God.

**Bhajan**: Devotional singing.

**Bal Vikas**: The educational wing of the Sathya Sai Organization whose goal is to foster spiritual development in children and teach them the basic human values: Truth, Right Action, Peace, Love and Nonviolence. Literal meaning "blossoming of the child."

**Bar & Bat Mitsvahs**: A boy (bar) or a girl (bat), 13 years old, who has reached the age of releigious majority, a ceremony marking the girl or boy taking on their responsibility toward God.

**Darshan:** Seeing a holy person; to see the form of the Lord and receive his blessings.

**Dharma:** The dictates of God, the duty of man, code of conduct or self-disciplinary rules, duty, obligation, codes of morality, righteousness.

**Dharmakshetra:** The abode of righteousness, purified area of virtue; the name of the temple for Sai Baba in Bombay.

**Dhobi:** A washerman.

**Diksha:** Steady pursuit.

**Easwaramma:** Sai Baba's mother.

**Hatha Yoga:** School of Yoga which emphasizes union with God through physical postures.

**Havuruh:** Lit., a fellowship. A small informal Jewish prayer group.

**Hevra Kadisha:** Lit., a holy society, those who ritually prepare the dead for burial in Judaism.

**Jai:** Victory

**Kabbalah:** Body of Jewish esoteric doctrine and lore.

**Karma:** Action; an inescapable obligation or duty that has to be performed due to past deeds; destiny or fate written by one's own hand.

**Kepah:** Skull cap.

**Kohum:** "Who am I?"

**Kurukshetra:** The camp of the wicked egoistic Kauravas, field of action.

**Leela:** God's sport, God's divine play.

**Lingam:** Symbol of creation, symbolizes the form of God, as in the Shivalingam, the merging of the form with the formless. Because of the oval shape of the lingam, there is no beginning or ending, so it merges with the formless.

**Mahavakya:** A sanskrit word meaning a great saying. The word is used for divine aphorisms in the ancient Indian scriptures, like 'that thou art,' which convey the eternal truth.

**Mandir:** Temple.

**Namasmarana:** Incessant remembrance of the name of the Lord.

**Nishkamakarma:** Action, without any desire for the fruit of the action.

**Paramatma:** Creator, the Reality, the Universal Absolute, the Lord.

**Prema:** Pure love, love toward all with no blemish or attachment.

**Puja:** Ritual worship.

**Punja:** Merit acquired by means of good activity.

**Puttaparthi:** The village where Sathya Sai Baba resides, where his ashram is located.

**Rajasic:** The active, passionate aspect of nature.

**Ramakrishna:** A great saint that lived in the early part of this century.

**Ramana Maharshi.** A great saint that lived in the early part of this century.

**Sadhana:** Spiritual practice.

**Sadhu:** A holy man, generally used with reference to a monk.

**Samithi:** A center.

**Sanathana Sarathi:** "The Eternal Charioteer," the name of the ashram monthly magazine.

**Sanyasi**: One who has renounced everything, given up all desires in order to attain liberation. **Sanyas** is the path of renunciation.
**Sarva Dharma:** The symbol of the unity of faiths.

**Satsang:** Gathering in the company of good people.

**Sattwic:** The pure, calm and unruffled aspect of nature.

**Seva:** Service.

**Shakti:** The great universal energy. The great mother, consort of Siva. Siva and Shakti are inseparable aspects of the one Reality.

**Shivah:** The seven day mourning period, after a Jewish person dies.

**Shivaratri:** Literally, "the night of Siva," A time of austerity and intensified spiritual practice on that night in the lunar calender when the moon is smallest and furthest from the earth, therefore enabling spiritual aspirants to steady their minds and achieve liberation.

**Sloka:** Verse form of the Sanskrit epics.

**Sohum:** "I am God."

**Sruthis:** Scriptures.

**Sthithprajna:** One whom is neither inflated by joy nor depressed by sorrow, one who is stable in the knowledge of the atma only.

**Swami:** Lord, Master, spiritual perceptor.

**Tallit:** Prayer shawl.

**Tamasic:** The dull, slothful and inactive aspect of nature.

**Tefillin:** Lit., Phylacteries, prayer amulets bound by leather straps to the forehead and left arm.

**Vahinis:** Vahini means stream. Books written by Sai Baba such as *Prema Vahini* which means stream of love.

**Vibhuti:** Sacred ash frequently materialized by Sai Baba.

**Yogi:** Contented, God-centered man who lives simply and practices the disciplines, physical and mental, of yoga.

# BIBLIOGRAPHY

Bhatia, Naresh. *Dreams and Realities, Face to Face with God.* Prasanthi Nilayam, India: Dr. Poonam Bhatia, 1994

Chibber, M.L. *Sai Baba's Mahavakya on Leadership.* Faber, VA, Leela Press, 1995

*Complete Works of Vivakananda, Volumes I - VIII.* Ramakrishna Mission, New York,

Covey, Stephen R. *7 Habits of Highly Effective People.* New York Simon and Shuster, 1990.

Devi, Indra. *Sai Baba and Sai Yoga.* Delhi, India: MacMillan Co. of India, 1975.

Gibran, Khalil. *The Prophet.* London, England: William Heinemann, Ltd., 1973

Hawley, Jack. *Reawakening the Spirit in Work: The Power of Dharmic Management.* San Francisco, CA: Brett Koehler Publishers, 1993

Hejmadi, D. *Sathya Sai Baba, Voice of the Avatar.* Prasanthi Nilayam, India: Sri Sathya Sai Books & Publications.

Hislop, John. *My Baba and I.* San Diego, CA: Birth Day Publishing,1985.

*Jnana Vahini.* Prasanthi Nilayam, India: Sri Sathya Sai Books & Publications Trust.

Kasturi, N. *Loving God.* Prasanthi Nilayam, India: Sri Sathya Sai Books & Publications Trust, 1985.

_____.*Sathyam Shivam Sundaram.* 4 volume biography. Prasanthi Nilayam, India: Sri Sathya Sai Books & Publications Trust, 1981

Mason, Peggy. *Embodiment of Love.* London, England: Sawbridge Enterprises, 1989.

Howard Murphet. *Walking the Path With Sai Baba (Invitation to Glory).* York Beach, ME: Samuel Weiser, 1993.

_____.*Sai Baba - Man of Miracles.* York Beach, ME: S a m u e l Weiser, 1973.

_____.*Sai Baba Avatar.* San Diego, CA: Birth Day Publishing, 1980.

Prabhavananda, Swami. *Bhagavad Gita.* Hollywood, CA: Vedanta Press, 1987.

Prabhavananda, Swami. *Upanishads.* Madras, India: Sri Ramakrishna Math, 1968.

Sandweiss, Samuel H. *Sai Baba, The Holy Man...and the Psychiatrist.* San Diego, CA: Birth Day Publishing, 1975.

*Sananthana Sarathi.* Shivaratri Discourse. 1994

Sathya Sai Baba. *Dharma Vahini.* Comp. N. Kasturi. Prasanthi Nilayam, India: Sri Sathya Sai Books & Publications Trust, 1982.

Sathya Sai Baba. *Dhyana Vahini.* Comp. N. Kasturi. Prasanthi Nilayam, India: Sri Sathya Sai Books & Publications Trust, 1984.Sathya Sai Baba. *Sathya Sai Speaks, Volumes I-XI.* Comp. N. Kasturi. Tustin, CA: Sathya Sai Book Center of America, 1975

Sivanananda, Swami. *Self-Knowledge.* Sivanandanagar, India: Yoga Vendana Forest University, 1958.

Stearns, Jess. *Yoga, Youth and Reincarnation.* Garden City, New York: Doubleday, 1965

Sathya Sai Baba. *Summer Showers In Brindavan, 1990, 1993.* Prasanthi Nilayam, India: Sri Sathya Sai Books & Publications Trust, 1972.

## Other Books about Sai Baba

Baskin, Diana. *Divine Memories.* San Diego, CA: Birth Day Publishing, 1990.

Hislop, John. *Conversations with Sathya Sai Baba.* San Diego, CA: Birth Day Publishing, 1978.

Krystal, Phyllis. *Sai Baba - The Ultimate Experience.* Dorset, England: Element Books, 1985.

Mazzoleni, Don Mario. *A Catholic Priest Meets Sai Baba.* Faber, VA: Leela Press, 1993

Roof, Jonathan. *Pathways to God.* Faber, VA: Leela Press, 1991.

Sandweiss, Samuel. *Sai Baba: The Holyman... and the Psychiatrist.* San Diego, CA: Birth Day Publishing, 1975.

Sathya Sai Baba. *Indian Culture and Spirituality*. Prasanthi Nilayam,
   India: Sri Sathya Sai Books & Publications Trust, 1990
Warner, Judy. *Transformation of the Heart*. York Beach, ME:
   Samuel Weiser, 1990.

These publications may be purchased at local Sai Baba centers, in certain well-stocked bookstores, or by writing to:

Sathya Sai Book Center of America
305 West First Street
Tustin, California 92680

Bhagavan Sri Sathya Sai Baba's address is:

Prasanthi Nilayam P.O.
Anantapur District
Andhra Pradesh 515134
INDIA